RU
his
meaning 'wisdom of the human being'. As a
highly developed seer, he based his work on
direct knowledge and perception of spiritual dimensions. He initiated a modern and
universal 'science of spirit', accessible to anyone willing to
exercise clear and unprejudiced thinking.

From his spiritual investigations Steiner provided sugges-
tions for the renewal of many activities, including education
(both general and special), agriculture, medicine, eco-
nomics, architecture, science, philosophy, religion and the
arts. Today there are thousands of schools, clinics, farms and
other organizations involved in practical work based on his
principles. His many published works feature his research
into the spiritual nature of the human being, the evolution of
the world and humanity, and methods of personal development. Steiner wrote some 30 books and delivered over 6000
lectures across Europe. In 1924 he founded the General
Anthroposophical Society, which today has branches
throughout the world.

KUNDALINI

Spiritual Perception and the Higher Element of Life

RUDOLF STEINER

Compiled and edited by Andreas Meyer

RUDOLF STEINER PRESS

Translated by M. Barton

Rudolf Steiner Press
Hillside House, The Square
Forest Row, RH18 5ES

www.rudolfsteinerpress.com

Published by Rudolf Steiner Press 2019

Originally published in German under the title *Kundalini, Geistige Wahrnehmungskraft und höheres Lebenselement* by Rudolf Steiner Verlag, Basel, in 2017

A catalogue record for this book is available from the British Library

Print book ISBN: 978 1 85584 558 9
Ebook ISBN: 978 1 85584 504 6

Cover by Morgan Creative
Typeset by DP Photosetting, Neath, West Glamorgan
Printed and bound by 4Edge Ltd., Essex

Contents

Introduction

The very word 'kundalini' has a dazzling sound, drawing the interest of many people today even if they do not quite know what it means. It may suggest snake motifs, dancing dervishes or ancient sacred rites. Equally, many will regard it with prejudice, connecting the term with ideas about yoga, tantric practices or magic rituals, almost exclusively related to eastern traditions. The whole subject is often enveloped in vague mystery rather than founded on sure knowledge. And little attention has been given to Rudolf Steiner's preoccupation with the theme of kundalini and the references to it in his work. This is largely because he no longer used the word at all after 1909, replacing it with other terms subsequently found throughout his work. A closer study of these matters shows that Steiner in fact opened up an entirely new outlook on the whole complex of kundalini and its development, along with related teachings about the chakras, developing it further and integrating it into anthroposophic insights into human nature.

The present volume contains all relevant comments and notes by Steiner on the theme of kundalini, and for the first time highlights how this concept evolved in his thinking and what importance he accorded it. At the same time it accentuates the differences and similarities between the western path developed by Steiner and other, eastern paths, in the process revealing what was new and original about his schooling path.

Steiner described kundalini energy as early as 1903. At the time, his accounts were somewhat unusual in the West. Helena Petrovna Blavatsky had previously introduced the term into theosophical literature, referring to it in her book *The Secret Doctrine* (1888) without however offering further explanations.[1] Indian Sanskrit texts on kundalini[2] were not yet known in Europe at this time, the sources only becoming available in 1918 when translated by Arthur Avalon (the pen-name of Sir John Woodroffe). Later the subject was taken up again in Charles Webster Leadbeater's theosophical work *The Chakras* (1927).[3] Subsequently Carl Gustav Jung studied kundalini,[4] and Lama Anagarika Govinda[5] publicized it in the West in his book *Foundations of Tibetan Mysticism* (1956). Before Steiner though, neither the systematic development of the chakras nor methods for awakening kundalini energy had been described in detail.

The term kundalini, or also 'kundali' comes from the Sanskrit and means, roughly, 'ringed', 'coiled up' or 'coiled together'. As 'coiled up' or 'sleeping' power, it refers on the one hand to the creative power within us in general, and on the other it is one of various Indian designations for the occult power that is also called 'snake fire' or 'snake potency'. According to Avalon,[6] kundalini is seen as the 'foundation of all yogic practice' and as the 'mightiest manifestation of creative energy in the human body', which sustains the life of all earthly beings.

From 1904 to 1906 Steiner used the terms 'kundalini', 'kundali', 'kundalini light' and 'kundalini fire' in his lectures and books. Light is seen as the symbol of wisdom, and warmth as that of love. The kundalini polarity manifests in light and warmth, or wisdom and love, and thus in that spiritual 'power of perception' whose right awakening—in connection with the development of astral organs of perception (lotus flowers)—is the precondition for spiritual seership. For this reason, while he used the term, Steiner spoke both of kundalini 'fire' and 'light'.

Between 1904 and 1905 in issues 13–28 of the journal *Lucifer-Gnosis*,[7] Rudolf Steiner published the essays which he then compiled in the book *Knowledge of the Higher Worlds* (1909). In this book, and in all subsequent editions, the passages where mention was originally made of 'kundalini', 'kundalini light', and 'kundalini fire' were replaced by the terms 'power of perception', 'higher life element', 'organ of perception' and 'element of higher substance'. It therefore seems as if the whole theme of kundalini vanished from Steiner's works from 1909 onward. But in fact, in altered form, it continues to pervade his accounts of the schooling path, corresponding to western idioms and gradually evolving anthroposophic teachings about the human being.

To make clear the nature of the revisions undertaken by Steiner, we cite passages below from *Knowledge of the Higher Worlds* (GA 10), with the altered phrase in italics followed by the original version from *Lucifer-Gnosis*.[8]

Thus we see in what way the esoteric pupil has really become a new person by attaining this stage, only gradually maturing to the point of governing the *true higher life element* (the 'kundalini fire' as it is known) through the currents of their etheric body, and thus gaining a high degree of freedom from their physical body.[9]

Once the esoteric pupil has succeeded in attaining this life in their higher I then—or in fact already while acquiring higher consciousness—they are shown how to awaken to existence the *spiritual power of perception* (the 'kundalini fire' as it is known) within the organ created in the heart region, and conduct it via the currents characterized in previous chapters (issues). This *power of perception* (this kundalini fire) is an element of higher substance issuing from the said organ and streaming in luminous beauty through the revolving lotus flowers and the other channels of the developed etheric body. It radiates from there outward into the surrounding world of spirit and renders it spiritually visible, in the same way as sunlight falling upon objects from without makes them physically visible.

Only gradually in the course of development itself can we come to understand how this *power of perception* (this kundalini fire) is engendered in the heart organ. (This understanding is a subject of esoteric schooling itself. Nothing is communicated publicly about it.)

The world of spirit only becomes clearly perceptible as objects and beings to someone who in this way can send the *organ of perception* as we have described it (kundalini fire) through their etheric body and into the outer world in order to illumine such objects. From this we can see that full awareness of an object of the world of spirit can only arise when a person themselves casts the light of spirit upon it. In truth, the I that engenders this *organ of perception* (kundalini light) is not within the physical human body at all but, as we have shown, outside it. The heart organ is only the place where a person kindles this spiritual light organ (fire) from without. If we did not do so here but elsewhere, the spiritual perceptions thus arising would have no connection with the physical world. But we do need to relate all higher spiritual elements to the physical world, and by so doing allow them to work into the latter. The heart organ is precisely what enables the higher I to make the sensory self into its instrument, and the place from where this is governed.[10]

The second passage comes from the chapter headed 'Changes in Dream Life During Esoteric Training', whereas the corresponding essay in *Lucifer-Gnosis* (issue 24, May 1905) was still called 'Awakening the Kundalini Fire'.

The reason for these changes must doubtless lie above all in the fact that Steiner wished to shed the term of its connotations of eastern yoga,[11] and place it into a theosophical-anthroposophical context. Elsewhere, in connection with development of the 'sixteen-petalled lotus', Steiner explained how he saw the relationship with Buddhist teachings:

People well-versed in these matters will recognize in the conditions for developing the 'sixteen-petalled lotus' the instructions which the Buddha gave his disciples for their 'path'. Yet it is not a matter here of teaching 'Buddhism' but of describing developmental conditions that arise from spiritual science itself. That they accord with certain teachings of the Buddha cannot mean that they are not also *intrinsically* true.[12]

In Steiner's works, the theme of kundalini is inseparably connected with the development and configuration of the 'lotus flowers' or chakras. The inner practices[13] that lead to their awakening in our astral organization are likewise described in detail in his schooling book *Knowledge of the Higher Worlds*. From a certain stage of self-development these include exercises for self-knowledge and moral self-perfection that enable us to perceive the character and illusion of what we have previously regarded as our own I. The 'preparatory' or 'subsidiary' exercises, as they are called— corresponding to the eightfold path of the Buddha and the eight Beatitudes of Christ—are primarily described in the two books *Knowledge of the Higher Worlds* and *Occult Science, an Outline*, as well as in many lectures.

The awoken lotus flowers become organs of perception in the course of further schooling, initiating the process that leads to the birth of the higher I, the 'embodiment' of the higher in the lower self. This 'new self', governed by the higher I, then develops the capacity to autonomously guide the kundalini fire as the 'true higher life element'. It creates in the region of the heart an organ of light, superordinate to the chakras, as a luminous etheric centre. With this it can then guide and govern the kundalini force as 'spiritual power of perception'. This consciously governed power of perception, the kundalini fire, illumines the world of spirit in the same way that sunlight illumines physical objects. This brings about a reversal in the soul faculties of thinking, feeling and will:

> The moment kundalini is awoken, passive thinking
> becomes active, and active will becomes passive.
>
> We can describe this moment of awakening by saying
> that our inner *being* acquires an active, i.e. productive
> thinking, and a passive, i.e. receptive will.[14]

The many meditations given by Steiner are an aid in this
transformative process. Our capacity to perceive the spirit is
acquired through transformation and metamorphosis of soul
faculties into organs of perception for the supersensible.
When as spiritual pupil we become able to withdraw the
kundalini fire voluntarily from the organism, it becomes
possible to free ourselves from the physical body 'as if this
were no longer present'.[15] We can then voluntarily govern
from within what hitherto streamed into us and governed and
determined us from without.

According to Indian yoga teachings the kundalini resides
in all of us at the lower end of the spine; it is symbolically
depicted as coiled and sleeping in the lowest chakra. Steiner
also repeatedly connected the snake symbol with the picture
of the caduceus or staff of Mercury (as symbol of human I
development)[16] and with the spinal cord:

> If you concentrate on your spinal cord for instance, you
> will in fact always see the snake. You may also dream of
> the snake, for this is the creature that was transposed out
> into the world at the time the spinal column developed,
> remaining at this stage. The snake is the spinal column
> transposed into the outer world.[17]

According to Indian tradition the kundalini chakra lies
between the six-petalled and ten-petalled lotus flower as a

kind of intermediate organ.[18] Somewhat diverging in position from this, in Steiner's works it corresponds to the organ which he calls the heart organ and etheric centre from which a network of rays issue to the various lotus flowers. In *Knowledge of the Higher Worlds* he gives the following account:

> The purpose of this development is to enable a focal centre to form in the region of the physical heart, from which streams and motions emanate in the most manifold spiritual colours and forms. In reality this focal centre is not a mere point but a very complex configuration, a wondrous organ. It shines and glimmers spiritually in the most varied hues, and displays forms of great regularity that can change with great rapidity. And other forms and currents of colour flow from this organ to the other parts of the body, and also beyond it, pervading and illumining the whole soul body. But the most important of these currents flow toward the lotus flowers, infusing their separate petals and governing their rotation; then from the tips of the petals they stream outward and lose themselves in external space. The more highly developed a person is, the greater is the periphery around them in which these currents spread.[19]

In his 1910 book *Occult Science, an Outline*, Steiner then describes the development of this heart centre as follows:

> In the region that roughly approximates to the physical heart, we become aware of a new centre in the etheric body which configures itself into an etheric organ.

Movements and streams pass from there in the most diverse ways to the various parts of the human body. The most important of these streams pass to the lotus flowers, permeate them and their separate petals and then pass on beyond the body, pouring out like rays into external space.[20]

In Hatha Yoga, kundalini is connected with the elemental human spine and with our strength of I and will power.[21] Steiner also speaks of these aspects of kundalini in the context of anthroposophy's view of the world and human nature, and in relation to further important aspects of schooling. In a lecture on 26 August 1913 in Munich, for example, he says:

The strengthened sense of I one develops is an inner stability which we could call an elemental spine. We need to have developed both: lotus flowers so that we can transform ourselves, and something resembling a spine in the physical world, an elemental spine, so that we can develop our strengthened I in the elemental world.[22]

As preconditions for supersensible experience, Steiner speaks here, as often elsewhere, of the need to strengthen soul life and of 'higher moral experiences' such as stability of character, inner assurance, tranquillity and courage. These latter are of great importance in the modern era, chiefly in relation to the connection of Lucifer and Ahriman with the lotus flowers and the elemental spine. Steiner expressly warns against awakening the lotus flowers and developing the elemental spine without sufficient efforts to achieve moral stability. The moment the lotus flowers have awoken, luci-feric and ahrimanic spirits seek to usurp them and the elemental spine by connecting the lotus flowers too closely with the elemental spine. This danger for higher develop-ment can be neutralized only by developing moral impulses and by inner cleansing (catharsis), without which a person would be chained and straitjacketed in egoisms and illusions.

The path to inner cleansing and self-knowledge is in turn connected with the kundalini power: 'Through the kundalini fire, as it is known, a person can observe themselves from within.'[23] Just as we only see objects in the physical sense world by virtue of reflected sunlight, the awakening of kun-dalini fire and kundalini light makes it possible to perceive soul qualities: 'The moment we are able to illumine the soul with the aid of kundalini light, it becomes visible like an object upon which the sun shines its light.'[24]

In the further course of schooling, kundalini becomes a light organ that also enables us to have vision of the world of spirit, 'illumining the things of the higher world just as the outer sun illumines sensory things and creatures'.[25] A third stage follows 'at which the "true I" awakens, the world-encompassing self-awareness which is able to receive the key to true knowledge'.

This relates at the same time both to an aspect of earlier mystery schoolings and to esoteric research practice. 'Old accounts [of human nature] were gained when pupils became visible to themselves through meditation, through inner enlightenment.'[26] A major aspect of these schoolings was the transformation of the sensual forces of sexuality into powers of love. The Dionysian mysteries are a well-documented example of European initiation connected with kundalini power.[27]

> Sensuality transforms into love: it spiritualizes and ensouls itself. And the god who, for the Greeks in the mysteries, was close to this power of sexual maturity was Dionysus.... The god Dionysus is the last-born of the gods; that is, the Greeks saw him as the one who had brought human beings to their present state of autonomy.... Dionysus is the creator of autonomy.[28]

Steiner sees the higher goal of this development in connection with overcoming the division of the sexes.

> The ascent of the human being occurs initially through the overcoming of physical love; secondly through regulation of the breathing process, in relinquishing oxygen, the life of the plant; and thirdly by developing the kundalini light whereby we give back the light reflected by the mineral kingdom.[29]

The discovery that a man's etheric body is feminine, and the etheric body of the woman is masculine, was for Steiner one of the most 'seismic inner soul experiences'.[30] But this polarity is found in the astral body too. Starting from his account of every person's astral body being hermaphrodite, with both a male and female half (the 'second half' of the astral body is feminine in a man and masculine in a woman), Steiner, in a notebook entry, situated the kundalini fire very precisely. According to this, the kundalini fire is 'the activity, initially warmth and light, which is kindled in the second astral body'.[31] In a sketch, Steiner drew the stream of kundalini forces rising to the heart centre. Our upper and lower aspects meet in this stream. According to this sketch, the new heart organ—expressly not identical with the heart chakra of the twelve-petalled lotus flower—is located between the ten-petalled and twelve-petalled lotus flowers. In Indian traditions this heart lotus flower occupies an independent position alongside the twelve-petalled lotus flower and is often referred to as the 'isle' or 'throne' of jewels, upon which the vision of the 'world teacher' is seen.[32] This points clearly to an affinity with the Christ mystery.

A further, subtle aspect of the kundalini fire is mentioned on only one occasion by Steiner, in a lecture he gave on 29 December 1903. He considers here what connects the astral body with the physical body and its organs when, during sleep, these two entities are detached from each other and the astral body is dwelling in the world of spirit. His answer runs as follows:

> There is a kind of bond, a connection, which is a transitional matter between physical and astral matter. And this is called the kundalini fire. If you look at a sleeping person, you can always trace the motion of the astral body in the astral: you have a luminous streak leading to where the astral body is. You can always locate this place. As the astral body moves farther away, the kundalini fire becomes correspondingly thinner, forming an ever more tenuous trail and increasingly coming to resemble a fine mist. If you observe this kundalini fire very carefully, you will see it is not uniform. Some places within it are more luminous and dense, and these are the

points that lead the astral back to the physical. Thus the optic nerve is connected to an astral nerve by a denser part of the kundalini fire.[33]

These comments by Steiner accord in turn with the description of the 'sutratma' in the *Upanishads*, where this luminous streak is also called a 'silver thread'.[34]

The awakening of the kundalini fire is for Steiner predicated upon further progress on the path of schooling founded, as he repeatedly reiterates, on necessary preconditions. He describes how we with our western consciousness can achieve awakening of the kundalini—after first properly developing the lotus flowers—in the chapter of *Knowledge of the Higher Worlds* entitled 'Changes in Dream Life', and also in notebook entries.[35] But it should be noted that he only publicly communicates a part of this process of awakening, concealing other aspects or presenting them only in the context of his work as an esoteric teacher. Thus, in the original version of the text on awakening the kundalini fire in *Lucifer-Gnosis*, he explicitly states 'Nothing of this is publicly communicated.'

The same is true of the account of the lotus flowers he gives in connection with kundalini. Thus he says in relation to higher knowledge:

> The first stage . . . is connected with the development of the 'lotus flowers' as they are called, the sacred wheels or, in Indian terminology, the chakras, which are situated at very specific points in the body. Seven such astral organs are distinguished: the first, the two-petalled lotus flower, is close to the root of the nose; the second, the

sixteen-petalled, lies at the level of the larynx; the third, the twelve-petalled, at the level of the heart; the fourth, the eight- to ten-petalled, close to the navel; the fifth, the six-petalled, somewhat lower down; the sixth, the four-petalled, the swastika, is connected with all fertilization; the seventh cannot be spoken of without deeper elaboration. These six organs have the same significance for the soul world as the physical senses have for our perception of the sense world.[36]

In a note from 1906,[37] Steiner describes how the idea of the 'higher self' as life stream should be guided along the spine and connected with the kundalini power. The currents along the spinal column there described are referred to as occult arteries (*nadi*) in Indian Hatha Yoga.[38] Three of these are of particular importance for our understanding of kundalini: *ida* (bluish in colour, to the left of the spine), *pingala* (reddish in colour, to the right of the spine) and the life stream *sushumna* (in the centre)—the latter only developing during schooling. *Ida* and *pingala* intersect repeatedly, giving rise in relation to the central stream to the picture of the staff of Mercury, the caduceus. The dangers and one-sided tendencies of Lucifer and Ahriman, represented in the left and right streams, are reconciled through a Christian principle in the central one (*sushumna*).[39] This 'path of the centre' is therefore also to some degree pursued in eastern traditions.[40]

Pursuing the path from above downward, starting with thinking and the realm of cognition, and passing from there to the life centre, we can connect this with the biblical image of the Tree of Knowledge. The opposite path, from below upward, is by contrast connected with the Tree of Life. Kundalini initiation alters and completes the initiate's configuration of supersensible bodies by reintegrating the qualities of the Tree of Life that were lost at the Fall.[41]

In contrast to most yoga traditions which cultivate the life energy rising from the lower life centre, the western, Christian schooling path embodied by Steiner starts in our upper centre of consciousness, in thinking and the I. From there, the heart centre is then first developed.

What is called the 'etherization of the blood' underlies this path. From the heart, light-filled, etherized blood rises to the head region. There, in connection with the pineal and pituitary glands, it becomes an active energy by means of which, according to Steiner, we can redirect our thoughts into the lower, living realm of metabolism. The etherized blood here helps to free our thoughts from egoism and dependency on the physical organs so that they become capable of perceiving reality:

> Just as in the region of the human heart a continual transformation of the blood into etheric substance takes place, so a similar process occurs in the macrocosm. We can understand this if we direct our gaze to the Mystery of Golgotha, and to that moment when the blood of Christ Jesus flowed from his wounds.[42]

In accounts from the Indian tradition, a description is usually given of how the life stream (kundalini) is guided from the lower organs (the four-petalled lotus flower or kundalini snake) along the 'elemental spine' to the kundalini chakra; and from there runs independently of the elemental spine to the twelve-petalled lotus in free, spiralling coils. In Hatha Yoga the life streams continue further, beyond the two-petalled lotus, and unite in the 'thousand-petalled lotus' at the roof of the skull through which the soul of the yogi then departs from the physical body.[43]

The fact that Steiner says practically nothing about the 'four-petalled lotus' (root chakra)[44] likewise indicates that the Western, Christian path he embodied starts from the pole of consciousness, the realm of thinking and the two-petalled lotus. From there the centre of experience is shifted down-ward from the head to the heart. After development of the new heart centre as he describes it, forces can be guided consciously and, through specific exercises, the 'kundalini snake' can be fully awoken. In the process, the etheric heart organ assumes a mediating role as organ of perception between our upper and lower poles, forming a single con-figuration with the pole of consciousness and the chakras belonging to it. The Egyptian image for an initiate who has awoken the serpent power and is able to master it fully and consciously, is the pharaoh with the cobra head over his head. In Greek sculptures, too, the engagement of outstanding or heroic figures with the snake and its forces is depicted in numerous images.

In his book *The Serpent Power*, Avalon mentions that there was also a school of yoga in India in which development of the kundalini started above, with the two-petalled lotus.[45] But we must remember that in early yoga schools—and also still very often today in the modern 'esoteric scene'—awak-ening of the energy centres was, and is, focused chiefly on the human organism in order to develop certain (old) forms of clairvoyance or in order to use these forces to sustain the development and health of body and soul.

Steiner's innovation and merit lies above all in his refashioning of this path to accord with humanity's evolution of consciousness, founding it on an anthroposophic understanding of human nature. He did not however simply adopt a traditional doctrine and translate it into new terms, but formulated it anew based on his own experiences and research. One example at least should be offered here from his autobiography to demonstrate this. There Steiner explains how the reversal of thinking and will described above occurred in him:

> I felt how the ideational nature of my life hitherto receded in a certain manner, to be replaced by the element of will. For this to happen the faculty of will must be able to refrain from all subjective volition in the development of knowledge and perception. The will increased to the degree that ideation decreased. And the will also took over the spiritual perception that previously had been accomplished almost exclusively by ideation.[46]

Humanity's evolution into the *consciousness soul* means that our relationship with the body has entirely altered, but also that our consciousness is a thinking one. In the development of school-age children, life forces are transformed into powers of picturing and thinking that serve the activity of cognition. Later, in adulthood, meditation follows as a continuation of the evolution of consciousness and our developing humanity. Steiner repeatedly pointed out that detailed study of spiritual-scientific texts is necessary as a preparation for developing supersensible organs, in order to develop a strengthened, pure thinking on the one hand, and on the other to acquire orientation for subsequent spiritual perceptions. This schooling of thinking is an indispensable preparation for all attempts to engage in spiritual perception; and it is a widespread misconception that this is unnecessary, or even that ordinary, intellectual thinking is already in itself pure, sense-free thinking.[47] We can be guided here by the maxim that 'we only know the true power of thought if we experience it as it arises'.[48]

For Steiner, the development of the chakras and kundalini through meditation and spiritual schooling always serves to develop organs of perception and—on the foundation of human freedom—thinking consciousness, to a degree where this becomes capable, firstly, of spiritual self-knowledge, and secondly of conscious I experience. The principles of this modern schooling path therefore include the condition 'that someone who practises it does so in full consciousness. They should undertake and practise nothing whose effect they are not fully aware of'.[49] In this respect too the path developed by Steiner diverges from many practices in modern esotericism.

The schooling path that leads from above downward, through meditation in connection with further exercises, integrates free life forces and energy streams into processes of cognition, so that our full freedom is retained along with full control of these forces and processes of consciousness. A further characteristic of the path of schooling developed by Steiner is that spiritual experiences (spiritual vision and experience) are immediately comprehensible and transparent, and do not need to be retrospectively grasped or interpreted. There is therefore a simultaneity of spiritual perception and cognition. Experiencing and knowledge, *dhyana* and *prayana*, appear together in this form of 'knowing meditation', thus also in turn avoiding the dangers of spiritual vision without insight, or knowledge without direct experience. This quest for 'knowing meditation' was described already in the history of Zen Buddhism.[50] Its application to the schooling path of chakras and kundalini as described by Steiner is, in this form however, entirely new and future-oriented.

Adaptation of the path of schooling to humanity's current evolutionary conditions also brings with it a new understanding of, and correspondingly a new way of relating to, our breathing. In pre-Christian time the spirituality wholesome for human beings was still connected with inhaled air and the breathing process whereas, since the Mystery of Golgotha, this spirituality has withdrawn from the atmosphere and now increasingly lives in the element of light. Activating the kundalini energy from below upward in pre-Christian yoga traditions was, accordingly, an 'air-soul process'. Steiner contrasts this with the impulse for a new, future-looking 'yoga will' in the form of a 'light-soul process'. The modern path of kundalini schooling is therefore no longer founded on respiratory processes but on our engagement with light via sense perception.[51]

Detaching the awakening of kundalini from the context of a properly understood and systematically undertaken schooling, along with mistaken, or mistakenly applied methods—especially a neglect of self-knowledge, of purification and of moral schooling—can render the kundalini energy very dangerous. The problem is exacerbated if 'awakening exercises' are done by people who are not mentally sound or who use these powers for egoistic purposes, for instance to enhance their sexual pleasure. In quite a few instances people develop severe psychological and psychosomatic conditions in consequence, or may even end up in psychiatric care. Their proper treatment would require a spiritualized medicine and spiritual psychology which, through precise understanding of these forces, and by specific perception of the loosened configuration of supersensible bodies, could reintegrate these again. Research and practice in this field is however still in its infancy.[52]

We can see that Steiner's elaboration of the kundalini theme is innovative especially in the polarity referred to earlier between light and love, or light and warmth. Steiner emphasizes that these two poles belong together at higher realms of human life as the two most important laws of earthly existence, comparable to positive and negative electricity or positive and negative magnetism. They are of fundamental importance for our inner development. The following notebook entry by Steiner also highlights this:

This physical body is built up by the powers of the astral body which goes as far as to create sense organs. These—the eyes—see objects by virtue of the outward sunlight. Within the astral body we have to distinguish a second half, like the other pole in a magnet. In a man, the second astral body is feminine, and in a woman, masculine; in other words, the astral body is hermaphrodite. The kundalini fire is in fact the activity—initially warmth and light—that is kindled in the *second* astral body. Until the kundalini fire is activated we only *feel* our way between the thing and beings of the higher world, as we might in the night between physical objects. Once the kundalini fire is present, we ourselves illumine things.[53]

If we study Steiner's work through to the late lectures and texts of 1924, or in the *Leading Thoughts* until 1925, it becomes apparent how prevalent is the theme of light and love (or warmth). It must be seen as a central theme of anthroposophy. Steiner's accounts culminate in this statement and question: 'Those who seek to grasp things through spiritual science, must ask first and foremost: How [in any phenomenon] are love and light interwoven, and to what degree?'[54]

Corresponding to this central importance, we find that some of the most significant meditations which Steiner created are founded entirely on the light-love polarity. We can reflect here on a meditation that is frequently referred to in relation to development of the lotus flowers, 'In the pure rays of the light [. . .] / In pure love for every being . . .';[55] or on the formulation given in the first mystery play, *The Portal of Initiation,* 'The weaving being of light shines forth / through breadths of space . . . Love's benediction warms / the cycles of passing time. . . .'[56]

In the fourth section of the Foundation Stone Meditation, we read: 'Divine light, / Christ Sun, / O warm our hearts; / Illumine our heads [. . .]';[57] and in what is called his 'last address', on 28 September 1924, Steiner gave the meditation

'Spirit forces springing from / sun powers', which is also reprinted in this volume.[58]

In *The Portal of Initiation*, the polarity of light and love comes to the fore once again in the final scene, when Johannes Thomasius says to 'the other Maria':

> I was not able to find the path
> To your higher sister
> As long as warmth of love in me
> Kept separate from love's light.
> The offering which you bring to the temple,
> Let it be recreated in my soul.
> Therein let warmth of love
> Offer itself up to the light of love.[59]

The great tension in this polarity has to be resolved by a free, harmonious relationship between the sensory and the supersensible. This corresponds to the words which Steiner has Maria say to her 'sister in sacrifice', the other Maria:

> Thus will we serve the great works of the cosmos
> When my light illumines your warmth
> And your warmth makes my light a fruitful thing.[60]

The two Maria figures in a sense correspond to the 'lily' and the 'green snake' in Goethe's *Fairy-tale of the Green Snake and the Beautiful Lily*. The lily represents the realm of the supersensible, the snake that of sensory existence.[61] In Goethe's tale the snake itself forms the bridge between the two realms: by sacrificing itself, the snake—as a picture of the soul's life experience—no longer leads a 'personal life' and is no longer oriented only to the sense world. Life experience has given rise to living wisdom, transforming into a soul capacity which we do not as such 'consciously practise but which acts only when the sensory and supersensible in our interior life mutually illumine and warm each other'.[62] Steiner characterizes this snake as a representative of the kundalini serpent energy. In his essay *The Chymical Wedding of Christian Rosenkreutz* (1917/1918),[63] he describes the serpent energy as an 'activity of the body of formative forces' which can be compared with the 'activation of radiating light'. The snake's self-sacrifice, which is at the same time connected with the secret of gold, consists in the metamorphosis of the serpent power to become an organ of perception for the spirit, thus building the bridge between the sensory and supersensible world.

In summary we can see that the kundalini theme is of vital importance in Steiner's work. Hella Wiesberger noted accordingly:

> From only a few exercises, albeit also in many different accounts of the spiritual-scientific path of schooling, it is apparent that all the exercises serve first and foremost to develop astral organs of perception, the 'lotus flowers' as they are known, and the awakening of what is called the 'kundalini fire'.[64]

Proper awakening and integration of the kundalini energy is important not only for those who seek to perfect themselves through meditation and spiritual schooling, but is above all a necessity of soul health. Precisely because the configuration of our 'bodies' or levels of being is loosening in the modern era, leading to the unleashing of sexual forces, we need a schooling that can help cultivate ongoing healthy human evolution. In a lecture he gave on 28 October 1904 in Berlin, Steiner therefore emphasized that, in our contemporary cultural epoch, the kundalini fire must flow into the realm of 'conscious, rational life':

> This is a power that at present still slumbers in the human being, but will come to be of ever greater importance. Today it already has a great influence, great importance, in what is perceived through the sense of hearing.[65]

Wrongly awoken—especially when this happens through methods that neglect a necessary moral purification—the serpent energy becomes a threatening power. There are many sad instances of this in modern esotericism. But developed by the right means, it can be a benevolent light-bringer for us, like Goethe's 'green snake' in his fairy-tale or Steiner's 'other Maria' in the mystery play. The raising of the snake then occurs with clear and conscious powers.

The biblical image of Moses 'raising the snake' in the wilderness shows this to be a profoundly Christian motif. Christ speaks of it in his conversation with Nicodemus: 'And as Moses lifted up the serpent in the wilderness, even so must the Son of man be lifted up: That whosoever believeth in him should not perish, but have eternal life.' (John: 3:14–15)

As long as the kundalini power remains inactive, as latent potentiality in the depths of the organism, at the life pole, it is experienced as 'kundalini fire' and has an affinity with the warmth-ether. When it enters the sphere of the centre, our rhythmic system—that of the central lotus flowers—it expresses itself as resonant life, connected with the inter-acting light- and tone-ether. In the upper sphere, in the region of the life-ether, kundalini manifests as light. Thus a uniting of the four ether types occurs. Kundalini awakens when we hear inner resounding, the inner word, first as fiery energy, then as word and tone, and finally as light. Christ is the source of the word, tone and light. Light and warmth in the physical world are connected with the spiritual light and spiritual warmth which we can find when we experience the Christ as spiritual sun within us.

At the same time, the kundalini power is connected with a key theme of the future: in the next cultural epoch, the sixth, 'this kundalini fire will gain great influence upon what lives in the human heart'. The new etheric heart organ that can already be developed through spiritual schooling in the present era—at the level of Inspiration, and as a hearing of 'inner tone' and 'inner word—will then have developed in many people, and will have been lit by the awoken kundalini fire:

> People will then be pervaded by a special power living in their hearts, so that, in the sixth root race, they will no longer distinguish between what serves their own good or what serves the good of all. They will be so imbued by the kundalini light that they will possess the principle of love as their most intrinsic nature.[66]

In the seventh cultural epoch a small proportion of human beings will then belong to those who are 'the true sons of the kundalini fire'. The goal of evolution is for the kundalini fire 'to kindle, with sacred pathos, the divine principle within human beings, so that person and person will no longer be separated but, so far as thinking intelligence extends, fraternity will have been achieved'.

In the same lecture, Steiner indicates that the kundalini principle is only slowly 'working its way through' and for now is still 'veiled and concealed by human beings' 'sundering passions' and the 'dividing forces of karma'. As long as the kundalini power as 'divine fire' has not yet become 'divine love', it manifests as 'divine anger'. But 'this divine fire, which contains the power of fraternity, and which will revoke and redress our separateness' can today already be developed through initiation.

Andreas Meyer

1. The Meaning of Meditation, and the Six Exercises

The aim of contemplation (meditation) on the symbolic thoughts and feelings characterized above is, to be precise, the development of higher organs of perception within a person's astral body. These are first created out of the substance of this astral body. These new organs of perception mediate a new world, and within this we learn to know ourselves as a new I. These organs differ from the organs with which we observe the physical sense world already in the fact that they are *active* organs. Whereas eye and ear behave passively and let light and tone act upon them, we can say that the soul-spiritual organs of perception are continually active and in a sense *encompass* the things and realities they perceive with full consciousness. This gives rise to the feeling that soul-spiritual cognition involves uniting with these realities, a 'living within them'.

We can call the separately forming soul-spiritual organs by the metaphorical designation of 'lotus flowers', which corresponds to the form that supersensible awareness must (imaginatively) conceive them to be. (But naturally we should remember that this designation is only figurative.) By very specific forms of inner contemplation we act upon the astral body to develop one or another soul-spiritual organ, one or the other 'lotus flower'. After all that has been described in this book, it should be superfluous to stress that these 'organs of perception' are not to be conceived in sensory terms. These 'organs' are of course supersensible, consisting in a specifically configured activity of soul; and they exist only in so far and for as long as this soul activity is performed. These organs in us are as little sensory in nature as would be some kind of 'thirst' in us when we think. Those who try to conceive of the supersensible in very sensory terms will succumb to misunderstanding.

(Occult Science, an Outline, 1910)[67]

Please note this point particularly: in meditation and focused contemplation, our aim and endeavour is always first of all to avoid living in ordinary egoity, and its mediation of physical experiences. Instead we seek to press this egoity down into the astral body, where it is not initially reflected in the physical body. When you look at a bunch of flowers, you are in reality within it. The physical body is a reflecting apparatus, and you see the bunch because the physical body reflects it to you. If you suppress the I and egoity, then you will be within the astral body—and this is so fine in nature that you can consciously perceive subtle, fluctuating things, but for this to happen, if you are truly to perceive them, they must also first be reflected. Now this is something you must very carefully consider: there are many among you who assiduously and faithfully practise meditation. By means of this practice you succeed in suppressing ordinary egoity and begin to have experience within the astral body. But reflection of it is still needed to consciously perceive in the astral body. There are indeed a whole host of you who, in your practice of meditation, have reached the point of experiencing within the astral body. But now what matters is the reflection. And just

as the physical body reflects back to us what we experience in ordinary life, so, if we wish to consciously perceive in the world of spirit, we first have to receive the experiences of the astral body through the etheric body.
(Dornach, 3 October 1914)[68]

The theosophist says: 'Today I am at a certain stage of human cognition, at which I can perceive this or that, and fail to perceive this or that.' But it is possible to develop this human power of cognition itself, to enhance it. Schools of initiation, as they are called, basically exist to raise this human faculty of perception to a higher level. Thus at a lower level of cognition it is actually quite correct to say that there are limits to knowledge, and there are things we cannot know or perceive. Yet we can also raise ourselves beyond such a level and reach higher stages of knowledge; and then we become able to perceive things which we could not know at lower stages. This is the very nature of initiation, and this deepening or raising of knowledge is the task of initiation schools. It is a matter of raising people to stages of knowledge that they cannot reach by nature alone, but must first gain through long, patient years of practice.

Such schools of initiation have existed in every era. People in every culture have emerged with higher, enhanced perception from such schools. And the nature of these schools of initiation and of the great initiates themselves who have grown beyond lower levels of human cognition, becoming aware through the inspirations they gained of the highest forms of knowledge possible on this earthly globe, comes to expression in the fact that these initiates endowed the various peoples of the earth with their many different religions and worldviews.

Today, in broad outline, let us reflect on the nature of these great initiates. Just as in every discipline, in every intellectual procedure, we must first acquire the methods that allow us to develop knowledge, so the same is true of schools of initiation. Here too certain methods lead us toward the higher stages of knowledge I spoke of. I now intend briefly to describe the stages involved in this. Certain stages of knowledge can only be achieved in the intimate surroundings of initiation schools—only where there are teachers who have themselves first passed through this schooling and faithfully practised such exercises, and therefore can properly assess each and every step on the way. And it is only to such teachers that people should entrust themselves in a school of initiation.

But it must be said that there is no such thing as 'authority' in such schools, nothing dogmatic: the principle holding sway in them is merely an advisory, counselling one. Someone who has undergone a certain methodical path of learning to acquire experiences of higher, supersensible life, knows how intimate are the ways that lead to this higher knowledge. Only such a person is qualified to say what is necessary in this realm. The only indispensable quality in the relationship between pupil and teacher is that of trust. Without it you can learn nothing. But with trust you will very soon see that an esoteric teacher will not advise you to do anything other than what they themselves have undergone. The principle at work in schooling is that only the outer, visible form of the human being is today already in finished form. Otherwise—and everyone who seeks esoteric schooling must recognize this—a person standing before us today is not finished and complete but developing, and in future will attain higher stages.

The aspect of us which has already become 'God's likeness', and therefore now stands at the highest level, is our sensory body, the part that we see visibly before us, or in general perceive through our senses. But this is not our only aspect. Our nature also has higher elements: firstly, the one that we call the etheric body. Someone who has developed their soul organs can see this etheric body. By virtue of it we are not just a configuration of chemical and physical forces but a living entity that grows, lives and can reproduce. This etheric body, which represents a kind of archetype of the human being, can be seen if we 'suggest away' the ordinary physical body by using methods of the art of clairvoyance which will be further described below. As you are aware, using ordinary methods of hypnosis and suggestion you can tell someone that this lampstand here, for instance, is actually not there, and then the hypnotized person will no longer see it. Similarly, by developing sufficiently strong willpower you can divert attention away from the physical body so thoroughly that although you are still looking into physical space, you can suggest away this physical space completely. Then, rather than seeing empty space, you will see it filled with a kind of archetype. This archetype has roughly the same form as the physical body but is not completely the same in nature. It is, rather, a thoroughly organized entity. It possesses not only a network of fine vessels and currents, but also has organs. This entity, this etheric body, is what makes us living beings. Its colour can be compared only with that of newly-opened peach blossom—it is not a colour in the solar spectrum, but is somewhere between violet and pink. So this is our second body.

The third body is the aura, which I have often described, a cloud-like form . . . in which we exist as within an egg-shaped cloud. It brings to expression everything living in us as desire, passion and feeling. Joyful, devotional feelings manifest in bright colour streams in this aura. Feelings of hatred and sensual feelings show themselves in darker colour tones. Sharp, logical thoughts express themselves in sharply out-lined figures whereas illogical, confused thoughts reveal forms with vague outlines. In this aura therefore we have an image of the feelings, passions and drives living in our soul.

The human being in the form I have now described was placed upon earth—as it were by nature's hand—roughly at the start of the Atlantean era. Last time I explained how this Atlantean era should be seen. At the point when fertilization with the primal, eternal spirit had already occurred, we have before us a human being with three aspects: of body, soul and spirit. Today this threefold human nature has already chan-ged a little since that time—since nature 'discharged' us—by virtue of the fact that we have become a self-aware being, have worked upon our nature. To work upon ourselves means to refine our aura, sending light into it from this self-awareness. Someone at, let us say, a primitive stage of development, who has not worked upon themselves, has an aura of the kind originally endowed by nature. But in educated and civilized circles, people have auras on which they themselves have already worked; for in so far as we are self-aware beings, we work on ourselves, and this work comes to expression initially in changes to our aura. Everything we have learned and assimilated since we have been able to speak and reflect in self-awareness has become a new quality in our aura that we ourselves have brought about.

Let us imagine ourselves back to the Lemurian era, when human beings had already had warm blood flowing in their veins for quite some time. They were fertilized with the spirit in the middle of this era. But they were not yet capable of conscious thought—evolution was only just beginning. The spirit had just taken possession of human corporeality. At that time the aura was still a natural endowment entirely. And then one could observe ... a smaller aura emerging, bluish in colour, inside the human head—that is, at a place we should locate within the head. This smaller aura is the outer, auric expression of self-awareness. And the more a person evolved this self-awareness through their thinking and work, the more this aura spread out over the other, so that they often both changed completely in a short time. Someone living as an educated person in outer civilization is working on their aura in the way governed by this culture they live in. Our ordinary knowledge that we gain at school, the experiences that life brings us: we assimilate them and they continually change our aura. But these changes must be taken in hand and continued if a person is to embark on practical mysticism. Then we must especially work upon ourselves. Rather than just incorporating what our culture offers us, we must ourselves exert an influence upon our aura in a particular and proper way. And this is done through what we call meditation. Such meditation, or inner contemplation, is the first stage through which the pupil of an initiate must pass.

What is the purpose of meditation? It is worth trying to become aware of the thoughts you have from morning to evening every day, and to reflect on how your thoughts are affected by the time and place in which you live. See if you can prevent the thoughts you have, and ask yourself whether you would have the same ones if you didn't happen to live in Berlin at the beginning of the twentieth century. At the end of the eighteenth and beginning of the nineteenth centuries, people did not think in the same way as they do today. If you consider how the world has changed over the past century, and what kind of changes have arisen, you will see that what fills your soul from morning to evening depends on the place and time in which you live. But it is different if we surrender to thoughts that have eternal value. Really such thoughts are only abstract, scientific ones, the loftiest thoughts of mathematics and geometry. We can discover that these have eternal value if we give ourselves up to them. Two times two is four—this holds true in all eras and all over the world. The same applies to the geometrical truths we assimilate. But if we look aside from the sure foundation of such truths, we can say that the average person harbours very few thoughts that are independent of location and time. Things dependent on these factors connect us with the world and exert only a small influence on the enduring essence of our being.

Meditation means nothing other than surrendering to thoughts with an eternal value, so as consciously to educate ourselves in what lies beyond physical space and time. The great religious texts contain such thoughts: the Vedanta, the

Bhagavad-Gita, the Gospel of John, from Chapter 13 to the end, and also Thomas à Kempis's *Imitation of Christ*. Those who practise contemplation with patience and persistence so that they dwell in and upon such texts, repeatedly meditating each day, and perhaps working for weeks upon a single sentence, thinking through it and feeling it fully, will gain infinite benefit from this practice. Just as we can get to know and learn to love a child better every day, with all their idiosyncrasies, so we can allow an eternal phrase—one originating with the great initiates or inspired people—to pass through our soul repeatedly; and this will fill us with new life. The sayings in *Light on the Path* are also highly significant, transcribed by Mabel Collins from higher guidance. Just the first four are already suitable, if we contemplate them with the right patience, to affect the aura, to illumine it entirely with a new light. One can see this light gleaming and dawning in a person's aura. Reddish or reddish-brown shimmers of hue are replaced by blueish ones; likewise bright orange colours replace yellow ones, and so on. All the aura's colours alter under the influence of these eternal thoughts. A pupil cannot yet discern this to begin with, but will still nevertheless gradually begin to sense the profound effect that issues from this greatly altered aura.

If, in addition to such meditations, a person also conscientiously practises certain virtues, undertakes certain soul practices, their soul's 'sense organs' develop within the aura. We need these if we are to see into the soul world, just as we need physical sense organs to be able to perceive the physical world. Our outward senses were implanted into the body as a natural endowment. But we ourselves have to implant higher sense organs of the soul into our aura through regular practice. Meditation means that we mature to the point where we can, from within, develop the soul senses that are already present within us as potential.

But in order to do so we have to direct our attention to very particular inner practices. As I said, we have a potential range of such sense organs within us, called the lotus flowers—called thus because the astral configuration we begin to develop in our aura when we work upon it in the way described, assumes a form we can figuratively convey as lotus flowers. This is only metaphorical of course—rather like speaking of 'butterflies in the stomach'. The two-petalled lotus is in the centre of the forehead above the root of the nose and between the eyes. Close to the larynx lies the sixteen-petalled lotus. The twelve-petalled lotus lies in the heart region, and the ten-petalled close to the pit of the stomach. Lower down we find the six-petalled and the four-petalled lotus. Today I wish to speak only about the sixteen-petalled and twelve-petalled lotus flowers.

In the teachings of the Buddha you can read of the 'eightfold path'. You may wonder why Buddha specifies this eightfold path as being of special significance for achieving higher human evolution. The eightfold path consists of the following: right resolve, right thinking, right speech, right action, right living, right striving, right remembrance, right contemplation. Now a great initiate like Buddha does not speak out of some vaguely felt ideal but out of real knowledge of human nature. He knows what effect is exerted by such inner practices upon the bodies that will only develop in future. If we observe the sixteen-petalled lotus in an average person of today, we will see very little. If I can put it like this, it is only just beginning to dawn. In ancient, primordial times, this lotus flower was already present, but has regressed during human evolution. Today it is just beginning to reappear as a result of human culture, and in future it will once again fully unfold. Its sixteen spokes or petals will shine brightly, each petal appearing in a different tone of colour, and eventually it will revolve from left to right. What every person will one day experience and possess is already being consciously formed today by those who seek initiate schooling in order to become the leaders of humanity. Now, eight of these sixteen petals were already developed in the primordial past, while eight still remain to be developed if the esoteric pupil wishes to use these sense organs. These latter develop when a person pursues the eightfold path in a clear, attentive manner, consciously practising these eight soul activities taught by the Buddha and organizing all inner life in such a way as to undertake these eight virtues as vigorously as possible. An esoteric pupil who takes themselves in hand in this way, supports meditative work by so doing, and not only brings the sixteen-petalled lotus to maturity but also into motion, thus developing true perception.

I now want to speak of the twelve-petalled lotus, in the region of the heart. Six of its leaves were already developed in the primordial past, and the six others must develop in future in all people, but today already in initiates and their pupils. In all theosophical texts you can find mention of certain virtues to be acquired as preparation for attaining the level of a *chela* or pupil. These six virtues, found in every theosophical manual on self-development, are: control of thoughts, control of actions, forbearance, steadfastness, open-mindedness and equilibrium—or what Angelus Silesius calls composure. These six virtues, which must be consciously and assiduously practised alongside meditation, unfold the six other petals of the twelve-petalled lotus. This is not some blind or wilful matter, nor dictated by personal predilection, but originates in the profoundest knowledge of the great initiates. These initiates know that someone who really seeks to develop to higher, supersensible levels, must unfold the twelve-petalled lotus. To do so, such a person has to practise these virtues to develop, today already, the six petals that were not yet developed in the past. Thus you can see how the initiates gave their life-enhancing teachings out of a deeper knowledge of human nature. I could extend these reflections to other organs of knowledge and perception, but today this must suffice as I wish only to give an outline of the process of initiation.

Once the pupil has come to the point of beginning to develop these astral sense organs and thereby is able not only to see sensory impressions in their surroundings but also soul impressions, and thus what exists as aura in human beings, animals and plants, then a whole new level of instruction commences. Before someone's lotus flowers start to revolve, they cannot perceive anything of these soul impressions in their environment, just as someone without eyes cannot see colour or light. But having broken through the barrier, and advancing far enough at a preliminary stage of knowledge to be able to see into this soul world, then a person's real pupilship begins, and leads through four stages of knowledge. What happens at this point when, having completed the preparatory stages, someone becomes a *chela*? What we have so far described all relates to the astral body, as we have seen; and this is entirely organized by the human body. Someone who has taken these developmental steps now possesses a quite different aura. Having illumined their astral body through self-awareness and having themselves become the light-filled organization of their astral body, then we say that the pupil has illumined their astral body with *manas*. Manas is nothing other than an astral body under the sway and mastery of self-awareness. Manas and astral body are one and the same thing, albeit at different stages of development.

We have to recognize this if we wish to make practical use, in practical mysticism, of the seven principles referred to in theosophical manuals. All who are familiar with the path of development, all who understand initiation, will say that while these principles have a theoretical value for study, they are only valuable in practice if one understands the relationship between the lower and higher principles. No practical mystic is concerned with more than four aspects: the physical body, in which chemical and physical laws are at work, then the etheric body, then the astral body, and finally, self-awareness which, at our current evolutionary stage, we call *kama-manas*, or the self-aware principle of thinking. Manas is nothing other than what self-awareness incorporates into the body. As it is at present, the etheric body is unavailable to any influence from this self-awareness. We can indirectly affect growth and nutrition but not in the same way as we can allow our wishes, thoughts and ideas to issue from our self-awareness. We cannot ourselves directly initiate our nutrition, digestion and growth, which are not connected with self-awareness. Now this etheric body has to be brought under the sway of the astral body, the aura as we call it. The self-awareness of the astral body must permeate the etheric body, and be able to work upon it in the same way that a person works upon their aura in the manner described. When, through meditation, through inner contemplation and practice of the soul activities I described, a person comes to the point where the astral body has been independently organized, then the work transfers to the etheric body; and then the etheric body acquires the inner Word and we not only hear what lives in our surroundings, but the inner meaning of things also resounds in our etheric body.

I have often remarked here that what is truly spiritual in things is their sounding, resounding. I pointed out that the practical mystic, when he speaks accurately, speaks of a sounding in the world of spirit in the same way that he speaks of a shining in the astral or desire world. There is good reason why Goethe, in leading his Faust heavenward, says,

> The sun resounds in age-old way,
> its song competing in fraternal spheres,
> and its great journey preordained,
> in thunderous course it brings full circle here.

And likewise with good reason Ariel says, as Faust is conducted through the spirits of the world of spirit, 'For ears of spirit the new day's birth resounds.'

This inner resounding, which is of course not in sounds perceptible to the outer sense of hearing, this inner word within things, through which they express their intrinsic nature, is the experience we have when able to affect our etheric body from our astral body. And then we have become a *chela*, the true pupil of a great initiate, and can be led further upon the path. Such a person, having attained this level, is called 'homeless' because they have found a connection with a new world—because the world of spirit resounds to them, so that they no longer feel at home, really, in this world of the senses. But this should not be misunderstood. The chela who attains this stage remains just as good a citizen and parent, just as good a friend as they would have done if they had not become an esoteric pupil. There is no need for them to be sundered from any of these contexts of life. What they experience in this pupilship is a developmental path of the soul, upon which they acquire a new home in a world that underlies this sensory world.

What has happened here? The world of spirit sounds into them, and as it does so, they overcome an illusion—*the* illusion that grips all people before they reach this stage of development: the illusion of the personal self. People believe they are personalities, individuals sundered from the rest of the world. But a simple reflection could show them they are not an independent entity even in the physical realm. Imagine the temperature in this room were 200 degrees hotter than it is, none of us could carry on surviving here. The moment outer conditions change, the conditions for our physical existence are under threat. We are only a continuation of the outer world, and simply inconceivable in isolation from it. This is even truer in the world of soul and spirit. We see that the person, seen as self, is only an illusion, that we are part of overall divine spirituality. And here we overcome the personal self. Goethe expresses this in his 'Chorus mysticus' in the words, 'Everything transient is but a likeness'. Everything we see is only a picture of eternal reality. We ourselves are only a picture of eternal reality. If we relinquish our separate being—and through the etheric body, indeed, we live a separate life—then we have overcome outer, separate life to become part of all life.

Now something arises in us that we have called 'buddhi'. In practical terms we have achieved the stage of buddhi, a developmental stage of the etheric body in which it no longer brings about separate existence but enters into all life, universal life. Someone who achieves this has arrived at the second stage of pupilship: all qualms and doubts fall away, and we can no longer be either superstitious or doubtful. We no longer need to assure ourselves of the truth by comparing our thoughts with the external world, testing them against it, but then we live in tone, in the Word within things, and the nature of things sounds and resounds from their essence. Doubt and superstition no longer have a hold on us. We call this 'giving the key of knowledge to the pupil'. Having reached this level, a word from the world of spirit sounds into this world. The pupil's words then no longer reproduce what lives in this world but what comes from another world, which works into this world but cannot be seen with our external senses; and these words are messengers from the gods.

Once this stage has been achieved, a new one comes. A person then gains influence upon the immediate actions of their physical body. Previously they could only affect the etheric body but now they can influence the physical body too. Our actions inevitably set the physical body in motion.

What a person does is integral to what we call their karma, but usually people do not consciously work on this, and do not know how any action they do inevitably leads to an effect. Only now does a person begin to undertake actions in the physical world with conscious awareness of working on their karma: they gain influence on karma through physical actions. Now, besides the things of the world around resounding to them, they reach the point of being able to utter the true names of all things. At our present level of culture, people are able only to speak one such name, the name they give themselves: I. That is the only name we can call ourselves. If we contemplate this more profoundly, we can come to deep insights here, far beyond anything conventional psychology even dreams of. There is one thing that you alone can give the proper name to. No other person can say 'I' to you. And you must say 'you' to every other, as they say 'you' to you. Within each person is something that only each person themselves can give the name of 'I'. This is also why esoteric Judaism speaks of the 'inexpressible name of God', something that is a direct annunciation of God within us. It was forbidden to utter this name in an unworthy or unholy way, and thus there was a sacred awe, a profound significance, when this name was uttered by the esoteric teacher in Judaism. I is the only word that tells you of something that you can never encounter in the outer world. And in the same way that everyone can give this name only to themselves, so the esoteric pupil of the third degree can give to all things of the world the names revealed to them by Intuition. In other words, the pupil has been resolved and assimilated into the universal I and can speak out of this universal I. The pupil may say to each thing its deep, inmost name, whereas an average person today can only say 'I' to themselves. Once the *chela* has reached this stage, they are called a 'swan'. Those who can raise themselves to the names of all things are called 'swan' because they can announce and proclaim all things.

What lies beyond this third degree cannot be expressed in ordinary words, for it requires knowledge of a special script that is taught only in esoteric schools. The next degree is that of the one who is 'cloaked' or 'veiled'. Beyond this lie the degrees of the great initiates—those who have given great developmental impulses to culture in all ages. They were first *chelas*. First they gained the key of knowledge, and then were led to regions where the names of things were revealed to them. Then they raised themselves to the universal level, and had profound experiences that enabled them to inaugurate the world's great religions.

But as well as the great religions, every great impulse, everything that is important in the world, originated from the great initiates. Let me give just two instances of how the great initiates, who underwent esoteric schooling, have influenced the world.

Let us take ourselves back to the daily reality of times when initiation pupils were instructed under the guidance of Hermes. This instruction initially involved what was called an 'ordinary esoteric' or academic course of learning. I can only give a very brief outline of its contents. Pupils were taught how the universal spirit descends into the corporeal world, incarnates there, and comes to life within matter, then reaches its highest level in the human

being and celebrates its resurrection. Paracelsus, in particular, expressed this very beautifully when he said that
what we meet in the surrounding world, these diverse living entities, are separate letters, and the word that com-
bines them is the human being. We have discharged upon
the creatures of the world all human virtues or frailties. But
we are the confluence of everything. How a confluence of
the whole of the rest of the macrocosm lives in us human
beings as microcosm was taught as esoteric lore in all its
details, and with a huge wealth of insight, in the initiation
schools of Egypt.

Following this course of instruction came the hermetic
instruction. What I just described can be understood with
our ordinary senses and intellect. But the hermetic teachings
can only be grasped once we attain the first degree of
pupilship, where we learn the special script—one that is not
random or arbitrary but reproduces the great laws of the
world of spirit. Unlike our ordinary script, this is not an
outward reflection fixed arbitrarily in separate letters and
parts of speech but is born from the spiritual law of nature
itself. And this is because a person acquainted with it is in
possession of these natural laws. Thus the pupil's whole
thinking in soul and astral space itself becomes lawful, and
what they think and picture accords with these great symbols
of the script. This is possible by relinquishing the self, by
surrendering to ancient, eternal laws. Now the pupil has
undergone hermetic instruction and is admitted to the first
stage of a deeper initiation, where they are to experience
something in the actual soul world of a significance above
and beyond the cosmic cycles. After the astral senses have

come to full effect, so that these work down as far as the etheric body, the pupil is then led into a profound secret of the astral world over three days, experiencing there what I described to you last time as the origin of the earth and the human being. The pupil experiences and has before them this elaboration of the spirit, this separation of sun, moon and earth, and the emergence of the human being—this whole sequence of phenomena. And at the same time these phenomena stand before them as pictures. Then, after this great experience in the school of initiation, the pupil goes about among the people and tells them what they have experienced in this soul and astral world; and this account runs roughly as follows:

Once a divine couple, Osiris and Isis, were united with the earth. This pair are the rulers of all that happens on earth. But Typhon tracked down Osiris and hacked him into pieces, and Isis went in search of his corpse. She did not bring him home, but made graves for his dismembered parts in various places across the earth. And thus he has fully descended and is buried in the earth. But upon Isis a ray of the spiritual world fell, that fertilized her through immaculate conception so that she bore the new Horus.

This mythology was nothing other than a grandiose account of what we have heard here about the emergence of sun and moon, their separation and the rise of the human being. Isis is the symbol of the moon, while Horus signifies earthly humanity, the earth itself. In great pictures the pupil experienced what occurred in the soul world before humanity was endowed with warm blood, before it was as yet clothed in a physical body. At, respectively, the beginning of the Lemurian, Atlantean and post-Atlantean eras of evolution, the great initiates prepared humankind to receive these great truths in such pictures and myths. For this reason they were not simply presented in prosaic form but in the picture of Osiris and Isis. All the great religions we find in antiquity were first experienced by the great initiates in the soul world; and then they went forth and spoke to each group and nation in the way each could understand—that is, in pictures of what they themselves had experienced and witnessed in the schools of initiation. Only by passing through such a school of initiation could they rise to a higher astral experience of these things.

As Christianity emerged, things changed. This marks a decisive turning point in evolution. Since Christ's appearance it became possible to be 'naturally' initiated in the same way one speaks of poets who are 'naturally gifted'. There are Christian mystics who received initiation as an act of grace. The first to be called to bear the message of Christianity out into the world, in accord with the saying, 'Blessed are those who have not seen and yet have believed', was Paul. The vision on the road to Damascus was an initiation outside of the mysteries. There is no scope here for me to go into further detail on this.

All great movements and cultural impulses have been inaugurated by great initiates. A beautiful myth that seeks to show this has come down to us from the medieval period, at a time when people did not yet demand materialistic proofs. The epic I'm thinking of arose in Bavaria, and therefore assumed the mantle of Catholicism. We can understand what happened in the following way: In Europe, in those days, the culture of townships was developing, modern citizenship. Humanity's advancement, the progression of every soul toward a next stage, was something that the mystic saw in terms of the emergence of the soul, of our feminine aspect. The mystic sees the soul as something feminine, and as fertilized by lower, natural sense impressions and eternal truths. The mystic sees such fertilization occurring in every historical process. For someone who can delve deeper into humanity's evolution, who can see the spiritual powers underlying physical phenomena, the great impulses for humanity's advancement are given by the great initiates. Thus in the medieval period too, this ascent of the soul to higher levels during the new cultural era brought about by developing cities, was ascribed to the great initiates. This urbanization was achieved by virtue of the fact that the human soul was taking a leap forward in history, and this leap forward was brought about by an initiate. All great impulses were ascribed to the great lodge of initiates who surrounded the Holy Grail. From there came the great initiates, who were invisible for people in outward life. And the figure who at that time instigated urban culture was called Lohengrin in medieval times. He is the ambassador, if you like, of the Holy Grail, of the great lodge. And the soul of the cities, the feminine aspect, which was to be fertilized through the great initiates, is indicated in the figure of Elsa of Brabant. The mediator of this is the Swan, who brings Lohengrin over into this physical world. One must not ask the name of the initiate, since they belong to a higher world. The *chela*, the Swan, mediated this influence.

Here I can only outline the fact that a great impulse was

symbolically seen by people in terms of a myth. This is how
the great initiates worked, conveying in this form what they
wished to proclaim in their teachings. Those who founded
the originating cultures of humanity worked in a similar way:
Hermes in Egypt, Krishna in India, Zarathustra in Persia,
Moses amongst the Jewish people. And likewise Orpheus,
Pythagoras and, ultimately, the initiate of all initiates, Jesus,
who bore the Christ within him.

I have spoken here only of the great initiate figures, trying
to characterize here the nature of their connection with, and
effect upon, the world. My account may seem alien to many.
But those who have themselves gained an inner intimation of
higher worlds, always look up not only to worlds of spirit but
to the leaders of humanity. Only because of this could they
speak as enthusiastically as did Goethe. But there are other
figures too in whom you find a sacred spark that leads us to
this point which spiritual science seeks to revive. You can
find it in a young German thinker and poet whose life appears
like the blessed memory of a past life as a great initiate. If you
read Novalis, you will sense something of the lifting breeze
that wafts us into this higher world. In his own distinctive
idiom, he captures something that magic spells also have.
Thus he writes beautifully of the relationship between our
planet and humanity, which holds true as much for people at
a lower, undeveloped level as for the initiate. He says that
humanity is the meaning of our planet, the nerve connecting
this planet with the higher worlds; it is the eye by virtue of
which this planet gazes upward into the heavenly realms of
the universe.

(Berlin, 16 March 1905)[69]

The next condition pupils experience [following dreamless sleep and then one in which essential reality reveals itself to them] is what we call 'continuity of consciousness'. Ordinarily we are unconscious in sleep when we are fully removed from the sense world. But this is no longer so for those who attain the above stage: they then live uninterruptedly in full, clear consciousness, even when the physical body is resting. After some time our entry into a particular new condition is marked by the fact that tones and words are added to the pictures of waking consciousness. These pictures speak and tell us something; they speak a comprehensible language, saying what they are. No illusion of any kind is possible any longer. This is the resounding and speech of devachan, the music of the spheres. Each thing then utters its own name and its relationship with other things. This complements astral vision, and marks the clairvoyant's entry into devachan. Having reached this devachanian condition, the lotus flowers, chakras or wheels start revolving from left to right at certain places in the astral body, like the hands of a clock. They are the astral body's sense organs, but their form of perception is an active one. The eye, for instance, is at rest, allowing the light to enter it, and then perceiving it. The lotus flowers on the other hand only perceive when in motion, when encompassing their object. Through their rotation, resonances arise in astral matter, giving rise to perception on the astral plane.

But what are the powers that develop these lotus flowers? Where do they originate? We know that, during sleep, the depleted forces of the physical and etheric body are replenished by the astral body: during sleep its regularity can redress irregularities in the physical and etheric body. But these powers that are used to renew us when we are tired are the same ones that develop the lotus flowers. Thus a person at the beginning of their esoteric training is withdrawing regenerative forces from their physical and etheric body. If these forces were withdrawn permanently from the physical body, a person would fall ill and would succumb to complete exhaustion. To avoid physical and moral harm therefore, such forces must be replaced by something else.

It is important to remember a universal rule here: rhythm replaces strength! This is an important esoteric principle. People today live very irregular, arrhythmic lives, particularly in their thinking and actions. Someone who let the distractions of the outer world simply act upon them, and went along with them, would be unable to avoid the dangers to their physical body arising from the withdrawal of forces during esoteric development. For this reason, we must work to create rhythm in our lives. Naturally we cannot ensure that each day is exactly the same, but there is one thing we can do: we can undertake certain activities with great regularity each day. This is obligatory for us when we undergo esoteric development. So, for instance we should practise meditation and concentration exercises each morning at a time we ourselves determine. We can also bring rhythm into our lives by undertaking a retrospective review of each day in the evening. If we can introduce other such regular practices into our life as well, it will be all the better, for by doing so our life begins to accord with a universal lawfulness. The whole cosmos, after all, is rhythmic, as is everything in the natural world—the course of the sun, the passage of the seasons, day and night and so on. Plants grow rhythmically. However, as development ascends, the less we find rhythm in it, though even the life of animals is still marked by rhythm to some degree—animals, for instance, mate at regular times and seasons. Only the human being's life grows arrhythmic and chaotic; nature has, as it were, discharged us from her care.

But we must now shape this chaotic life rhythmically again. To achieve this we can find particular means to introduce harmony and rhythm into our physical and etheric body, so that these gradually come to resonate rhythmically and regularly. Then, when the astral body detaches itself from them, they can correct and remedy themselves. Though they may have been drawn into irregularity during the day, nevertheless this regularity of practice means that, during rest, they re-establish the right motions once again.

The means to do this are found in the following six exercises, which must be undertaken alongside meditation:

Control of thoughts. This means that, at least for brief moments in the day, we do not let all possible thoughts pass chaotically and at random through our soul but instead bring tranquillity into our thought processes. We think of a particular idea, and place this at the centre of our thinking, then develop from it in logical sequence all further thoughts so that they relate to the first. If we do this only for a minute or two, it is already of great importance for the rhythms of the physical and etheric bodies.

Initiative in actions. This means compelling ourselves to actions, even apparently insignificant ones, originating only in our own initiative; engaging in tasks we set ourselves. Mostly our actions are determined from without, by family circumstances, education, our profession and work, and so on. Just think how little we do actually arises from our own initiative! Therefore we must now take a little time to allow actions to proceed from our own initiative, unsolicited by outer factors. There is absolutely no need for these to be things of importance, for completely insignificant actions fulfil the same purpose.

Composure. This is the third thing we need: learning to regulate the swings in us between being 'over the moon' and 'down in the dumps'. If you decline to do this because you think it will impair your spontaneity or your artistic temperament, then it's better to refrain from the esoteric path. Composure, or equanimity, means keeping your centre through the greatest joys and profoundest pain. Actually, if you no longer lose yourself in utter pain or joy, if you no longer dissolve into them egoistically, you become truly receptive to joys and sufferings. The greatest artists have in fact attained the greatest composure because, in doing so, they opened up their soul to apprehensions of subtlety and importance.

Positivity. This fourth quality is one that sees the good in everything, invariably seeking the positive aspect in all things. There is a Persian legend about Christ Jesus which can offer us a fine example of this: Christ Jesus once saw a dead dog by the side of the road. He stopped and looked at it, whereas his companions turned away from it in disgust. But Jesus Christ said, 'Oh, what beautiful teeth the creature has!' He was looking beyond the ugliness of the rotting corpse to find something beautiful there, the white teeth. If we cultivate this mood, then we seek positive attributes, the good in everything; and we can find it everywhere if we look. This has a hugely powerful effect upon the physical and etheric body.

Belief. In its esoteric meaning, this next attribute, of belief, expresses something different from what people ordinarily mean by it. If we embark upon esoteric schooling, we should never let our past cloud our view of the future. Under all circumstances we should leave aside what we have previously experienced so as to meet each experience with a mood of faith. The esoteric pupil must do this consciously. If, say, someone came to you and told you that the local church tower had keeled over sideways to a 45° angle, almost everyone would say this was impossible. But the esotericist must allow a little window of possibility for everything, meeting every occurrence with an open mind, with belief; for otherwise we place obstacles in the way of new experience. We must continually be willing to meet with new experiences, and this engenders in the physical and etheric body a mood that can be compared with the voluptuous mood of a creature hatching an egg.

Inner equilibrium. This next quality gradually develops by itself through the five other attributes. A person must be conscious of, and attentive to these six qualities. We must take our life in hand, and slowly progress, remembering the old saying: the stone is worn by steady drips.

If, without taking account of this, a person acquires higher powers by some kind of magical intervention, they will be at grave risk. In contemporary life the spirit and the body are intermingled rather like a blue and yellow fluid in a jar. With esoteric development something begins that resembles the process a chemist undertakes to separate these two fluids.

Soul and body are similarly separated, but this means a person loses the benefits of the mix. In ordinary life, people are not overly subject to the sway of grotesque passions for the very reason that their soul inhabits the body. But as a result of this separation the physical body can be left to its own resources, with its particular attributes, and this can lead to all kinds of excess. If someone pursuing esoteric development does not take care to cultivate moral qualities, bad attributes that would not otherwise have become apparent can manifest: they may suddenly become deceitful, given to outbursts of anger, vengeful; all possible traits that were once modified or moderated manifest in a crass form. In fact, this can even occur if someone concerns themselves too intently with the wisdom and teachings of theosophy without at the same time developing themselves morally.

(Stuttgart, 2 September 1906)[70]

2. Developing and Cleansing the Lotus Flowers

Thus the first stage is that of Imagination, connected with development of what are known as the lotus flowers, the sacred wheels or—in Indic—the chakras, situated at specific points in the body. Seven such astral organs are distinguished: the first, the two-petalled lotus flower, close to the root of the nose; the second, the sixteen-petalled, lies at the level of the larynx; the third, the twelve-petalled, at the level of the heart; the fourth, the eight- to ten-petalled, close to the navel; the fifth, the six-petalled, somewhat lower down; the sixth, the four-petalled, the swastika, is connected with all fertilization; the seventh cannot be spoken of without deeper elaboration. These six organs have the same significance for the soul world as the physical senses have for our perception of the sense world. The symbol known as the swastika is an image of this. Through the exercises we have spoken of, these organs first become brighter then start to revolve. In modern people they are immobile. In Atlantean times they were still in motion, and in Lemurian times very vibrantly so. But in those times they rotated in the opposite direction from their motion today in a person who has developed esoterically, where they now turn in a clockwise direction. Analogous to the state of dreamlike clairvoyance of the Lemurians is that of mediums today in whom, similarly, the lotus flowers revolve in an anti-clockwise direction, as they did in Atlantean and Lemurian times. The clairvoyance of mediums is unconscious in nature, without control of thoughts, whereas that of the true clairvoyant is conscious and precisely governed by thinking. Mediumship is highly dangerous, whereas sound esoteric schooling is completely safe.

(Leipzig, 9 July 1906)[71]

Above all, through the etheric body's own intrinsic nature, the drive toward transformation awakens when we depart from the physical body and then, in our etheric body, have the elemental world as our environment. We desire to immerse ourselves in the beings there. But just as the need for sleep arises in waking life, so this desire alternates with the need to be alone in the elemental world, to exclude everything into which we might transform ourselves. Then in turn, when we have had the sense of being thrown back on ourselves for a while, when we have spent some time developing a strong sense of will to be ourselves, then something we could describe as a terrible sense of loneliness arises, a sense of being forsaken, which invokes the longing to awaken, as it were, from this state of desiring ourselves alone, and to become once more capable of transformation. In physical sleep we rest, and our forces ensure that we awaken without ourselves having to do anything to make this happen. But in the elemental world, when we have put ourselves into the sleeping state of desiring only ourselves, we must, when instigated to this by the sense of loneliness and forsakenness, return ourselves to the transformational condition and capacity—or in other words, we must decide to awaken. From all this you can see that conditions of self-experience, of self-perceiving, differ greatly in the elemental world from those in the physical sense world. And so you can gauge how necessary it is repeatedly to remember that clairvoyant consciousness, passing back and forth between one world and the other, really properly accommodates the demands of each world, rather than bringing the habits and customs of one world into the other with it each time it passes back and forth across the threshold. Strengthening and empowerment of soul life is therefore intrinsic to the preparations we have often spoken of for experiencing supersensible worlds. Strengthening and empowering of soul life.

Above all, soul experiences we can call higher moral experiences must become strong and vigorous—experiences that manifest in the soul mood of character stability, of inner certainty and tranquillity. Inner courage and stability of character must above all be developed in the soul, since weakness of character weakens our whole soul life, and this would mean we enter the elemental world with a weakened soul. This must not happen if we wish to have true and proper experience of the elemental world. And for this reason, no one who takes the experience of higher worlds seriously will ever fail to stress the importance of strengthening moral powers of the soul in order to enter into higher worlds in the right way. It is one of the most grievous errors, gravely misleading to others, to speak of acquiring clairvoyance without at the same time emphasizing the need to strengthen our moral character. It is important to remember that what I described in *Knowledge of the Higher Worlds* as development of the lotus flowers, these organs which crystallize as it were in the spirit body of the developing clairvoyant, can—but definitely ought not to—occur without recourse to strengthening of our moral nature.

These lotus flowers must be present if a person wishes to have the capacity for transformation, for the latter involves these organs unfolding their petals away from the human self and encompassing the world of spirit, leaning into it. The transformational capacity we develop expresses itself for clairvoyant perception in the unfolding lotus flowers. The strengthened sense of I one develops is an inner stability which we could call an elemental spine. We need to have developed both: lotus flowers, so that we can transform ourselves, and something resembling a spine in the physical world, an elemental spine, so that we can develop our strengthened I in the elemental world. Yesterday we spoke of how aspects which—spiritually developed—can lead to lofty virtues in the world of spirit, lead equally to the greatest vices if we allow them to flow down into the sensual world. The same is true of the lotus flowers and the elemental spine. It is possible to awaken both these through certain practices without first establishing our moral stability; but no conscientious clairvoyant will ever recommend this. You see, it is not just a matter of achieving this or that in respect of higher worlds, but of considering everything that is necessarily involved.

The moment we cross the threshold to the world of spirit, we come close to luciferic and ahrimanic beings, of whom we have spoken previously, in a way quite different from how we relate to them in the physical sense world. As soon as we cross this threshold, that is, as soon as we possess the lotus flowers and a spine, we see luciferic powers approaching us, and their aim is to grasp hold of the lotus petals: they extend their tentacles toward our lotus flowers, and we need to have developed in the right way in order to use these lotus flowers to apprehend spiritual occurrences, rather than allowing them to be misused by luciferic powers. But it is only possible to avoid this if we rise into the spiritual world with strengthened moral forces.

I have suggested already that in the physical sense world the ahrimanic powers approach us more from without, the luciferic powers more from within the soul. In the world of spirit, the reverse is true: the luciferic beings approach from without and seek to grasp hold of the lotus flowers, while the ahrimanic beings come from within and lodge themselves securely in the elemental spine. And now, if we have not ascended to the world of spirit with sufficient moral qualities, the ahrimanic and luciferic powers conclude a strange alliance with one another. While this is a figurative way of describing what Lucifer and Ahriman do, nevertheless the image I use corresponds to reality, and you will understand me. What I'm suggesting with this picture really happens: Ahriman and Lucifer form an alliance, a bond, connecting the petals of the lotus flowers to the elemental spine. All the lotus flower petals are fused with the elemental spine so that a person is straitjacketed, inwardly chained by their developed lotus flowers and elemental spine. And what this means is that egoism and love of deception occur to a degree inconceivable when we simply remain bound up with the physical world. This is what can happen when clairvoyant consciousness is not developed in the right way: Ahriman and Lucifer form a bond which fuses the lotus flower petals to the elemental spine, and thus one becomes chained by one's own elemental or etheric capacities. These are all things we need to know if we wish to try to penetrate with conscious perception into the real world of spirit.

(Munich, 26 August 1913)[72]

When the lotus flowers are developed without being informed by wisdom—Ahrimanic.

When their motion is developed without being informed by morality—luciferic.

Luciferic: the lotus flowers function, but they turn only to everything that accords with the personality; they turn toward our own ahrimanic element.

(Handwritten note, 1913)[73]

3. The Snake Symbol

While life in the physical body helps us develop earth consciousness, and dying into Christ substance helps us develop
post-mortem consciousness, we still lack knowledge of the self,
conscious self-awareness. We must be helped to develop this by
the messenger of the Christ, the Holy Spirit—*Per Spiritum
Sanctum reviviscimus*. Here the consonants predominate. The *p*
signifies placing and facing, the *s* signifies emergence from the
lap of the gods. When the *s* sound resounded through cosmic
space, the human spine was created. The wave-like surge of the
s is also the sign of Lucifer, in whose serpentine coils it is
reflected. If we succeed in overcoming him, we gain the
spiritual power that endows us with the right self-awareness:
Per Spiritum Sanctum reviviscimus.
(The Hague, 25 March 1913)[74]

In every course of esoteric teaching, it is important to learn
how we should look at the things around us. When looking at
a flower, and everything else in the environment, each person
naturally feels something or other. But it is a matter of
gaining a higher perspective, of gazing deeper, of connecting
certain perceptions with each thing. The profound medical
insights of Paracelsus were for instance based on this. He felt,
sensed, saw, the power of a particular plant and its affinity
with something within human beings. Thus for example he
saw what organ in us is affected by the power of *Digitalis
purpurea* (red foxglove).

Let us use a particular example to clarify this way of regarding things. All religions have symbols. We can hear much today about such symbols, but this is only external and arbitrary interpretation. The deep religious symbols, by contrast, are drawn from the very nature and essence of things. Let us consider for instance the snake symbol as this was taught to Moses in the Egyptian esoteric schools. Let us discuss what inspired him, what furnished him with Intuition.

There is a fundamental difference between all the animal creatures who have a spine and those that do not, like beetles, molluscs, worms and so on. We can divide the whole animal kingdom into vertebrates and invertebrates. In the case of the invertebrates we can ask where their nerves run, since vertebrates have the main nerve cord running of course through their vertebrae. Invertebrates also have a nervous system, which exists similarly in the human being and vertebrates, running outside and along the spinal column and extending from there to the body's cavities. We call this the sympathetic nervous system, with the solar plexus. This is the same system that invertebrates also possess, but it has less importance for vertebrates and the human being. It is a system that has a much closer connection with the rest of the world than the neural system in the head and spine. In a state of trance we can extinguish the activity of the latter, and then the sympathetic nervous system is activated—as we see for instance in sleep-walkers. The awareness of a somnambulist extends to the whole life around them, entering into other creatures. Somnambulists feel surrounding things within them. The life ether is the element that flows around us everywhere and is mediated by the solar plexus. If we were able only to perceive with our solar plexus, we would live in intimate community with the whole world, which is the experience of invertebrates. Such a creature feels a flower within it, for instance. In the earth's complex, the invertebrate resembles the eye and ear of a human being. It is part of an organism. In fact, there is actually a communal, spiritual organism that perceives through the invertebrates—sees, hears and so forth. The earth spirit is a communal organism of this kind. Everything we have around us is a body for this communal spirit. Just as our soul creates itself eyes and ears to perceive the world, so this communal earth soul creates the invertebrates as eyes and ears, in order to see into the world, and to hear into it.

Now there came a moment in the earth's evolution where an occlusion occurred in the common life of the earth spirit: a part of it secluded itself as if within a tube or channel. Only at this point did it become possible for creatures to emerge at all as separate entities. The others remained part of the earth soul, and only now did a special level of separation begin, with the growing potential for something eventually to say 'I' to itself. This fact of there being two epochs on the earth, firstly the one when there were no animals as yet with a nervous system enclosed within a bone channel, and secondly one when such creatures evolved, finds special expression in all religions. The snake first encloses the self-less, unified vision of the earth spirit within a channel and thus creates the foundation for egoity. The esoteric teachers impressed this upon their pupils by saying: Regard the snake, and you will see the sign and symbol of your I.

Thus they gained a vivid sense of how the autonomous I and the snake belong together. And so this feeling of the meaning of things around us was developed. In this way the esoteric pupils imbued every natural creature with the right content of feeling. Moses was equipped with this kind of feeling when he emerged from the Egyptian esoteric schools, and so he established the symbol of the snake. In these schools people did not learn in such abstract ways as today, but they learned, rather, to encompass the world out of their own inner experience.

Today we describe the human being based on external study of the separate parts of our organism. In ancient mystical and esoteric works, we can also find descriptions of the human being, but these arose in a quite different way from anatomical studies. They are actually far more precise and correct than what a modern anatomist describes, since the latter is concerned only with the corpse. The descriptions of antiquity were gained by students becoming visible to themselves through meditation, through inner illumination. Through what is known as the kundalini fire a person can observe themselves from within. There are various levels of such observation. Precise and correct observation first arises symbolically. If you concentrate on your spinal cord, for instance, you will in fact always see the snake. You may also dream of the snake, for this is the creature that was transposed out into the world at the time the spinal column developed, remaining at this stage. The snake is the spinal column transposed into the outer world. This figurative way of seeing the world is astral vision (Imagination). But only through mental vision (Inspiration) does the full meaning become apparent.

(Berlin, 26 September 1905)[75]

4. The Kundalini Fire

The third stage is to develop what is called astral seership. Then we can also see these auras. We see not only what is present in the physical world but also what exists in the astral world. When we reach this stage our astral aura changes somewhat. In people of the Atlantean and post-Atlantean eras, wheel-like figures appear within their astral aura; they exist in fact in the aura of every modern person. In Lemurian times they were as yet scarcely discernible. Seership begins for a person today when these 'wheels' start to revolve, while astral vision ceases when they are immobile. These are the three states.

A neural network runs through the physical body. Each nerve centre is connected with an astral centre so that, for instance the optic nerve is surrounded and enclosed by an astral optic nerve, an astral light substance that belongs to the optic nerve. How does vision arise? Light enters the eye, passes through the nerve into the brain. But as yet we see nothing—it is still only a physical movement process. But now the astral optic nerve starts to vibrate, and these reverberations give rise to the image that we see. Without activation of the astral body, it is impossible to see. The same is true of thinking. The astral body is the actual active element. If you now imagine what happens for seers, their perceptions are not impressions entering through the ears or eyes but ones that arrive through their astral organization itself, without mediation by the physical brain and the neural centre. This happens when the chakras, the lotus flowers are activated. And this means therefore, that the astral body is an organism possessing sense organs.

When we are in the normal state of sleep, the astral body is usually outside the physical body. The further a person develops on the path of self-development, the further the astral body can distance itself. Full psychic development involves us leaving the body behind and wandering around freely in the astral realm. There are further stages too. While we sleep, the astral body can undertake the strangest wanderings, though you don't remember these nightly travels. You may be aware of this during the night but not bring it to mind in the daytime. The highest stage is to be aware of astral consciousness both during sleep and also in the physical body. During the night you can visit people you know, though such experiences will not resemble the ones you have in the physical world. For example, you will not learn what a person is presently doing in Asia. But if you want to learn something from this person, you can do so if you bring it fully over into your waking consciousness. The *chela* could not learn whether a master in Asia is, say, writing or not writing, nor what he may be drinking or eating. But the one can teach the other in astral space and the chela can bring this back into waking consciousness.

If you look at an astral body, you have the physical body with its neural centres in one place, appearing physically as it does during the day, and then there is the astral body with its sense organs enabling you to see: the optic nerve belongs to this centre [of the astral body], as does the auditory nerve.

Now we can ask what connection there is between the

astral body and the physical body, what binds the astral ear to the physical ear. And why does the astral body [detached from the physical body during sleep] return? These are interesting questions. Let us assume, for instance, that someone felt terribly sad; then, during the night, they dwell in their astral body. Suffering and sorrow have their origin in the physical realm. The person might now decide not to return [from their astral body], and this would mean performing what would be called astral suicide.

What, then, connects the astral body with the physical body and its organs, and what leads it back to this connection? There is a kind of bond, a connection, which is a transitional matter between physical and astral matter. And this is called the kundalini fire. If you look at a sleeping person, you can always trace the motion of the astral body in the astral: you have a luminous streak leading to where the astral body is. You can always locate this place. As the astral body moves further away, the kundalini fire becomes correspondingly thinner, forming an ever more tenuous trail and increasingly coming to resemble a fine mist. If you observe this kundalini fire very carefully, you will see it is not uniform. Some places within it are more luminous and dense, and these are the points that lead the astral back to the physical. Thus the optic nerve is connected to an astral nerve by a denser part of the kundalini fire.

In his book [*The Astral Plane*], Leadbeater did not wish to engage with the subject of whether such astral suicide is possible or not. The kundalini fire with the astral body cannot be entirely lifted away from the physical body. If a person were to decide not to return, the kundalini fire would continually draw them down again; it is as if they still belonged to the physical body, following the trail of the kundalini fire. Until our life force has been entirely exhausted it is very difficult to raise the astral body out of the physical body. It is very difficult for someone to cling to the physical body they can no longer use. In this respect, the fate of the suicide and that of a person killed in an accident do not greatly differ from each other.

Now, in the case of a more highly developed person in whom the chakras revolve, another process occurs. Such a person will be able voluntarily to withdraw the kundalini fire from the organism, and at the same time opposing currents arise from within: what formerly streamed in is now something the person can regulate from within outward; the whole process can now be brought about intentionally. Thus we gain the capacity to govern the astral body fully. Please note that this condition is one that is increasingly arising in human evolution. Nowadays, psychically developed people have such an astral body, but human beings in general are rapidly tending towards such a state of affairs. In the sixth race they will gain the capacity to use their astral body. Within their physical body they will have an astral body that they can govern in this way. But in the next Round, humankind will no longer have a physical body, only an astral body that they can use freely and voluntarily in the same way that a person today can use their physical body. The physical body will then no longer exist; our lowest body will be the astral body.

In the mental body we find something that resembles the astral centres. The astral body has various sense centres: an astral centre corresponds to the optic nerve, as does another

to the auditory, and to the olfactory nerve and so on. The
mental body no longer has these separate senses, but only a
single one: it is imbued by the mental capacity of apprehension, and thus, with this single sense, it is able to perceive
mentally and so relate everything to everything else.

The rational capacity is the shadow of this mental sense.
When you hear a bell being struck, you are likely to turn
round so as to perceive what is happening visually too. The
astral senses are also connected to the mental sense by a kind
of kundalini fire. Thus the kundalini fire is a kind of intermediate substance that connects different conditions.
(Berlin, 29 December 1903)[76]

We see how the esoteric pupil really becomes a whole new
person by attaining this level [at which their higher self is
born to conscious existence]. They can now gradually
mature to the point of directing the actual higher life
element—'the kundalini fire'—through the currents of their
etheric body, and thus they attain a high degree of freedom
from the physical body.
(Lucifer-Gnosis, April 1905)[77]

Once the esoteric pupil has succeeded in developing this life
in their higher I, then—or in fact already while acquiring
higher consciousness—they are shown how they can awaken
what is called the kundalini fire within the organ created in
the heart region, and guide this through the currents
described in previous issues. This kundalini fire is an element
of higher substantiality issuing from the said organ, and
streaming in luminous beauty through the revolving lotus

flowers and also through the other channels of the developed etheric body. From there it radiates out into the surrounding world of spirit, and renders it spiritually visible in the same way that sunlight falling on objects from without renders these physically visible.

How this kundalini fire is engendered in the heart organ can only be disclosed in esoteric schooling itself. Nothing is communicated publicly about it.

The world of spirit only becomes clearly perceptible as objects and beings to someone who in this way can send the kundalini fire as we have described it through their etheric body and into the outer world in order to illumine such objects.

(Lucifer-Gnosis, May 1905)[78]

Within the astral body we have to distinguish a second half, like the other pole in a magnet.

In a man, the second astral body is feminine, and in a woman masculine; in other words, the astral body is her-maphrodite.

The kundalini fire is in fact the activity—initially warmth and light—that is kindled in the *second* astral body.

Until the kundalini fire is activated, we only *feel* our way between the things and beings of the higher world, as we might in the night between physical objects.

Once the kundalini fire is present, we ourselves illumine things.

(Notebook entry, 1905/06)[79]

5. The Kundalini Light

Everything that is now taught as anatomy alone was known in a quite different way back then. Esoteric investigators used the kundalini light in their enquiries. A pupil was prepared for this as follows. He came to the master and, if the latter acknowledged him to be reliable, he received instruction, but not in the form of a body of knowledge. Things are different nowadays: people must make their way through reason and concepts. Back then, instead, the master would say to the pupil something like this: each day you must spend several hours in meditation, initially for a period of six weeks, giving yourself up to one of the eternal sayings, immersing yourself in it entirely. A person cannot do such a thing today, since life in modern civilization makes too many other demands on us. Back then a pupil would meditate for six to ten hours a day. We could not do this without removing ourselves from the life around us. In those days the pupil needed to spend scarcely any time engaging with the life around him, but found his nourishment outside it. He therefore used his time for meditation, perhaps ten hours without interruption. This meant that he quickly brought his body—not yet so dense at the time—to a point where the kundalini light awoke within it. For our interior this is what sunlight is for the outer world. In reality we do not see objects as such outside us, but reflected sunlight. The moment we become able to use the kundalini light to illumine the soul, it becomes as visible as an object illumined by sunlight. Thus the whole inner body is

gradually illumined for the yoga pupil. All ancient knowledge of anatomy was perceived through this inner illumination. Thus the [Indian] monks, who couched their experiences in the form of legends, were speaking of what they had seen by means of the kundalini light.
(Berlin, 7 October 1905)[80]

The founding of new cities reached its peak in the fourteenth century. Within a few centuries, independent cities had arisen in all European countries. The citizen became the lynchpin of materialism in practical life, and this came to expression in the myth of Lohengrin. Logengrin, the ambassador of the lodge, was the wise leader who took a hand in developments in the medieval period and prepared the founding of cities. His symbol is that of the swan, signifying an initiate of the third degree. Consciousness is always depicted as something feminine. Elsa of Brabant represents the consciousness of materialistic urbanization. But spiritual life must be saved, and this is accomplished when Christian Rosenkreutz founds the Rosicrucian Order. Spiritual life was kept alive in the esoteric schools. Today, materialism has been driven to an extreme, and so a new intervention had to come in our era. The same movement that took a hand in those days now popularizes the basic teachings of spiritual life through theosophy in order to create a new inner life that can later manifest outwardly. Inner life always later manifests outwardly. An illness is the karmic consequence of a former misguided action, for instance a lie. When this takes effect in reality, it becomes an illness. Plagues can be traced back to long-past misdeeds of a people. They are something imperfect that shifts from within to an outward scenario.

The sixth sense is the kundalini light in a feeling of radiating warmth; the seventh is the sense of synthesis.
(Berlin, 4 October 1905)[81]

The world of spirit becomes clearly perceptible as things and entities only for someone who can send the kundalini fire through their etheric body out into the world in this way, thus illumining the things of that world. From this we can see that full consciousness of something in the world of spirit can only arise when a person themselves sheds spirit light upon it. In reality the 'I' that engenders this kundalini light is not within the human body at all but, as we have seen, outside it. The heart organ is merely the locus where a person kindles this fire from without. If they were not to kindle it here but elsewhere, then the spiritual perceptions engendered in this way would have no connection with the physical world. We need, however, to relate all higher spiritual realities to the physical world, and let them work through into it. The heart organ is precisely what enables the higher I to make the sensory self into its instrument, and the place where this is enacted.
(Lucifer-Gnosis, May 1905)[82]

The ascent of the human being occurs initially through the overcoming of physical love; and secondly through regulation of the breathing process, in relinquishing the life of the plant, of oxygen; and thirdly by developing the kundalini light, whereby we give back the light reflected by the mineral kingdom.
(Berlin, 6 May 1906)[83]

A person will then be pervaded by a special power that will live within their heart, so that, in the sixth root race, no distinction will be made any longer between their own good and the good of the community. A person will be so pervaded by the kundalini light that they will have the principle of love as their own, most intrinsic nature.

(Berlin, 28 October 1904)[84]

6. Developing the New Heart Organ

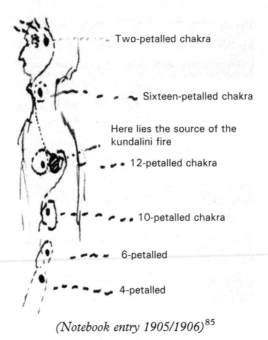

Two-petalled chakra

Sixteen-petalled chakra

Here lies the source of the kundalini fire

12-petalled chakra

10-petalled chakra

6-petalled

4-petalled

(Notebook entry 1905/1906)[85]

Development of the astral body . . . makes it possible for us to perceive supersensible phenomena. But if we really wish to find our way in that world, we should not stop at this stage of development. Mere rotation of the lotus flowers is not sufficient. A person must be independently able to regulate and control the motions of their astral organs in full awareness. Otherwise they would become a plaything of external forces and powers. If we are to avoid this, we must acquire the ability to hear what is called the 'inner word'. To succeed in this, not only the astral body but also the etheric body must be developed. This is the fine body that appears to the clairvoyant as a kind of double of the physical body. In a sense this is a transitional level between this body and the astral body. If you are gifted with clairvoyant capacities, you can, in full consciousness, 'suggest away' the physical body of a person standing before you. This is simply a higher level of ordinary concentration or attentiveness. Just as we can divert attention away from something in front of us so that it is not present to us, the clairvoyant can entirely extinguish perception of a physical body before them so that it becomes entirely transparent. If we do this with another human being, what remains before our soul gaze is the etheric body, as we call it, as well as the astral body, which is larger than both and also penetrates them both. The etheric body has *approximately* the same size and shape as the physical body, so that it takes up roughly the same space. It is an extremely delicate, finely organized configuration, whose basic colour is different from any of the seven colours of the rainbow. If you can observe it, you encounter a colour that is not really found in the sense world, and is closest in hue to young peach blossom. If you want to observe the etheric body on its own, then you also have to extinguish your perception of the astral body too, through an attention exercise similar in kind to the one described above. If you don't do this then the appearance of the etheric body is altered by the astral body infusing and pervading it.

Now in us human beings, the particles of the etheric body are in continual motion. Numerous currents pass through it in all directions. These currents sustain and regulate life. Every *living* entity has an etheric body of this kind. The plants and animals have it too. The attentive observer can even discern traces of it in minerals. These currents and motions are, initially, entirely independent of human will and consciousness, like the heart's activity or the stomach and digestion in the physical body. And as long as a person does not undertake schooling to acquire supersensible capacities, this remains so. You see, higher development at a certain level involves us complementing currents and motions that are independent of consciousness with ones that we ourselves bring about consciously.

By the point in esoteric schooling, described in previous issues, at which the lotus flowers start to revolve, the pupil will already have received instruction that leads to the eliciting of very particular currents and motions in their etheric body. The purpose of these instructions is to enable a focal centre to form in the region of the physical heart, from which streams and motions emanate in the most manifold spiritual colours and forms. In reality this focal centre is not a mere point but a very complex configuration, a wondrous organ. It shines and glimmers spiritually in the most varied hues and displays forms of great regularity that can change with great rapidity. And other forms and currents of colour flow from this organ to the other parts of the body, and also beyond it, pervading and illumining the whole soul body. But the most important of these currents flow toward the lotus flowers, infusing their separate petals and governing their rotation; then from the tips of the petals they stream outward and lose themselves in external space. The more highly developed a person is, the greater is the periphery around them in which these currents spread.

The twelve-petalled lotus flower has a particularly intimate relationship with this focal centre. The currents run directly into it; and currents pass through it to the sixteen-petalled and two-petalled lotus on the one hand, and on the other downward to the eight- six-, and four-petalled lotus flowers. This arrangement explains why very particular care must be given to development of the twelve-petalled lotus in esoteric schooling. If anything is omitted here, the whole development of the system would be awry. And this shows us in turn the delicate and intimate nature of esoteric schooling, and how carefully we must proceed if everything is to develop in the proper way. Inevitably this means that only those who have themselves experienced these things first-hand are in a position to give others instruction in the development of supersensible capacities, and likewise discern whether their instructions are having the proper and desired effect.

When the esoteric pupil carefully follows the guidance they are given, then they teach the etheric body currents and motions that are in harmony with the laws and evolution of the world to which we belong. For this reason, esoteric guidance and teaching is always a reflection of the greater laws of world evolution. It consists of very particular meditation and concentration exercises which, used in the right way, have the stated effects. The actual content of this teaching is only given individually during esoteric schooling. Each pupil must fill their soul entirely with a certain content at particular times, as it were imbuing themselves inwardly with it. Schooling starts with simple matters, suitable above all for deepening and internalizing the head's rational and reasoned thinking. This thinking is thus made free and independent from all sense impressions and experiences. It is, one can say, focused in a single point which we have entirely under our control. Thus an *interim* centre is created for all the etheric body's currents. This centre is as yet not in the heart region but in the head, and will be apparent there to the clairvoyant as the source of etheric motions. Schooling will only be fully successful if we create *this* centre first. If we were to transpose the centre to the heart straight away, the developing seer could, it is true, have certain glimpses of higher worlds but would not gain proper insight into the connection of these higher worlds with our sense world— something *indispensable* for people at the present stage of world evolution. The clairvoyant must not become a utopian dreamer, but must *always* keep their feet on the ground.

When this centre in the head has first been established firmly enough, it is transposed further downward, into the region of the larynx. This is brought about through further concentration exercises. Then the motions of the etheric body we have spoken of stream out from this region and illumine the astral space in a person's surroundings.

A further exercise enables the esoteric pupil to determine the position of their etheric body themselves. Previously this will have depended on forces coming from without and issuing from the physical body. Through further self-development a person becomes able to turn the etheric body in all directions, a capacity brought about by currents running roughly along our two hands, whose focal centre lies in the two-petalled lotus in the region of the eyes. All this comes about by virtue of the rays issuing from the larynx configuring into rounded forms, some of which pass to the two-petalled lotus flower and from there make their way as wavelike currents along the hands. A further outcome of schooling is that these currents branch and ramify in the subtlest manner to form a kind of membrane, a network encompassing the whole etheric body. Whereas previously the etheric body was not confined or enclosed, so that the life streams flowed directly in and out from the greater ocean of life, the influx from without must now pass through this membrane, and this means we become sensitive to these currents from without. They become perceptible to us. And the time has now come to transpose the whole system of currents and motions to the centre in the heart region. This happens again through a particular concentration and meditation exercise. And thus we also attain the stage at which we are endowed with the 'inner word'. All things now acquire new meaning for us. We can say that their inmost nature becomes spiritually audible to us—they utter forth their true being to us. The currents described connect us with the inner nature of the world to which we belong. We begin to indwell the life of our surroundings, and can let this life echo in the movement of our lotus flowers.

By doing so we enter the world of spirit. At this point we gain new understanding of what the great teachers of humanity spoke of. Buddha's discourses, for instance, now affect us in a new way—they pervade us with a bliss hitherto undreamed of, for the tenor of these words follows the motions and rhythms we have now developed within us. We can now have direct *knowledge* that someone like Buddha utters not his own revelations but those that flowed to him from the inmost reality of things. Here one fact should be noted, no doubt understandable only in the context now elaborated. People in our current era and culture do not properly grasp the many repetitions in Buddha's discourses. For the esoteric pupil they become something to dwell upon gladly with inner receptivity, for they correspond to certain motions of a rhythmical nature in the etheric body. Dedication to them in complete inner tranquillity also creates harmony with these motions. And since these motions are a reflection of certain world rhythms, in certain respects also involving regularity and repetition, as we hearken to the wisdoms of Buddha we enter into harmonious accord with world secrets.

Theosophical texts speak of *four* attributes which a person must acquire on what is known as the path of probation, in order to rise to higher knowledge. The first of these is the capacity to distinguish in our thought between the eternal and the temporal, the real from the unreal, truth from mere opinion. The second attribute is right esteem for the eternal and real as opposed to the transitory and unreal. The third capacity involves practice of the six attributes: control of thoughts, control of actions, perseverance, tolerance, faith and equanimity. The fourth is the quest for liberation.

Mere rational understanding of what lies in these qualities is of no use. They must be incorporated into the soul so as to establish inner *habits*. Take the first attribute, for instance: distinguishing the eternal from the transient. A person must school themselves so as to enable them to distinguish quite naturally, in everything they encounter, between what is transitory and what has lasting significance. We can only school ourselves in this way if, in great tranquillity and composure, we repeatedly and continually attempt to make such distinctions in our observations of the world around us. By so doing, eventually our gaze will as naturally find what is enduring in things as it previously made do with the transitory. The truth of the saying, 'Everything transient is but a likeness' will become the soul's self-evident conviction. And with similar persistence we must develop the other four attributes of the path of probation.

Now a person's fine etheric body is actually transformed under the influence of these four habits of soul. The first, 'distinguishing what is real from what is unreal', creates the focal point in the head and prepares the one in the larynx. However, the concentration exercises we referred to earlier are needed to *really* develop these centres, while the four 'habits' bring them to maturity. Once the centre in the larynx region has been prepared, what we described as free mastery of the etheric body, and its enclosure within a kind of meshwork, is brought about by right *esteem* of the eternal as compared to the transient. If we succeed in developing this esteem, higher realities gradually become perceptible to us. But we ought not to believe that only actions which rational assessment suggests are 'significant' should be undertaken. The least action, every smallest handshake, has significance in the great fabric of the universe, and it is simply a matter of *recognizing* this significance. It is important to rightly recognize the value of small daily actions rather than underestimate them.

We have spoken already of the six virtues that compose the third attribute.... These are connected with development of the twelve-petalled lotus flower in the heart region, toward which, as we described, the life stream of the etheric body must be directed. The fourth attribute, *the quest for liberation*, then serves to bring the etheric organ in the region of the heart to maturity. If this quality becomes a habit of soul, a person liberates themselves from everything connected *only* with the capacities of their personal nature. They cease to regard things from *their own* specific perspective. The boundaries of their narrower self, which shackle them to this perspective, now fade away. The secrets of the world of spirit gain entry to their inner being—and this is liberation, for these shackles compel us to regard things and beings in the way dictated by our own nature. The esoteric pupil must become *free* and independent of this personal way of regarding things.

From this we can see that the precepts originating from the great teachers of humanity have a deep and decisive effect that works through into our inmost human nature. And the doctrines on these four attributes issue, in the same way, from such 'primordial wisdom'. In one or another form we find them in every religion. The founders of these great religions gave these precepts to us out of far more than dim intimations; they did so consciously as great, enlightened initiates. They imparted their ethical precepts out of clear knowledge, knowing how these principles work upon human nature, and desiring their followers to slowly develop this finer nature. To live in accord with religions means to work at perfecting ourselves spiritually. Only when we do this do we also serve the whole world. To perfect ourselves is by no means self-seeking since an imperfect person is also an imperfect servant of humanity and the world. The more perfect we ourselves are, the better we can serve the whole. 'When the rose adorns itself, it adorns the garden too.' *(Lucifer-Gnosis, March 1905)*[86]

When a person has begun to develop their etheric body in the way described above, an entirely new life opens up for them. And, through esoteric schooling, they must receive elucidations at the right time that enable them to find their way in this new life. Through the sixteen-petalled lotus, for instance, the pupil will see the forms and figures of a higher world, and must recognize how different these forms are depending on their originating source or being. The first thing we can attend to is that our own thoughts and feelings exert a strong influence on the forms of a particular kind, but that they have little or no effect on others. Figures of the one kind alter as soon as the observer witnessing their emergence thinks, 'that is beautiful' and then, as they go on observing, changes the thought into 'that is useful'. The forms and figures originating in minerals or artificial objects have the peculiarity that every thought or feeling the observer brings to bear on them changes them. This is less true of the forms arising from plants, and still less so of those corresponding to animals. These forms are also mobile and full of life. But their mobility is only partly due to the effect of human thoughts and feelings upon them, and is partly also caused by aspects we cannot affect. Now, within this whole world of forms, a type of figure arises that is initially almost entirely unaffected by any human influence. The esoteric pupil discovers that these figures come neither from minerals, artificial objects, plants or animals. To be clear, these figures and forms are ones we find to be caused by the feelings, impulses, passions etc. of other human beings. But even these, as we discover, can be affected, although relatively little, by our own thoughts and feelings. Within this world of forms there is always also a residue upon which such influence is vanishingly small. And in fact, at an early stage of esoteric schooling, this residue forms a great part of what we see at all. And we can only gain insight into its nature by observing *ourselves*. We find that these forms originate in ourselves. What we ourselves do, desire, will and so on, comes to expression in them. An impulse that lives in us, a desire we have, an intention we harbour and so forth: all this manifests in such forms. In fact, our whole character expresses itself in the forms of this world. Thus, through our conscious thoughts and feelings we can exert an effect upon all forms that do not issue from ourselves, but the figures we give rise to in the higher world through our own nature are no longer subject to our influence once we have brought them into being.

From what has been said here, it is also clear that in higher vision our inner life, the world of our own impulses, desires and thoughts, manifests in outward figures in the same way as does that of other things and entities. For higher perception, our inner world becomes part of the outer world. It is like being surrounded on all sides by mirrors in the physical world, and so viewing our physical form outside us. In the higher world, similarly, our soul appears to us as mirror image.

At this stage of esoteric development, the point arrives when we overcome the 'illusion of the personal self', as theosophical texts put it. Elements within our personality can now be observed as outer world, in the same way that we observe the external world through our senses. Thus we gradually learn by experience to relate to ourselves as we have otherwise related to the beings around us.

If our gaze into this higher world were opened before we were sufficiently prepared for its nature, we would confront this portrait of our own soul as an enigma. The forms of our own drives and passions would appear to us in animal or— more rarely—human shapes. While the animal forms of this world are never identical to those of the physical world, they do bear a distant resemblance to them. Unpractised observers might well think them to be the same. Now, when we enter this world, we have to acquire a quite new kind of appraisal. Apart from the fact that the things that really belong to our inner life appear as outer world, they also manifest as the mirror image of their actual reality. If you see a number there, for instance, you have to read it in reverse. Thus 265 in fact signifies 562. You see a sphere as if you stood at its centre. And we have to translate this interior view of things in the right way. But soul qualities too appear here as mirror image. A desire that relates to something outside us appears as a figure moving toward us. Passions that have their seat in our lower nature can assume the form of animals or similar creatures attacking us. In reality these passions strive outward and seek the object of their satisfaction in the outer world. But this outward seeking appears in a mirror image as an attack upon the person whose passion it is.

If, before embarking on higher vision, the esoteric pupil has become acquainted with themselves through calm, objective self-observation, then, when they encounter the outward mirror image of their inner life, they will find the strength and courage to deal with this in the right way. But those who have not sufficiently acquainted themselves with their own inner nature through such self-examination, will not recognize *themselves* in their reflection, and think it instead to be a reality outside them. The sight of it will also cause them fear and, being unable to endure it, they will persuade themselves that the whole thing is just a product of fantasy, and of no benefit. In such cases, because of reaching a certain developmental stage without the maturity needed for it, a person will prove to be a disastrous hindrance to their own higher development.

It is absolutely necessary for the esoteric pupil to pass through spiritual sight of their own soul in order to penetrate to higher matters. Within our own soul, after all, we have the soul-spiritual aspect that we can best appraise. If we have *first* gained hard-won knowledge of our personality in the physical world, and then encounter the *image* of this personality in the higher world, we will be in a position to compare the two. We can relate the higher element to something known to us, and will therefore have sure ground under our feet. But however many spirit beings we otherwise encountered without this, we would be unable initially to understand their quality and nature, and would feel no sure foundation. It therefore cannot be sufficiently emphasized that sure and certain entry to the higher world must pass through sound knowledge and appraisal of our own nature and being.

Thus we first encounter *pictures* upon our path into the higher world, for the reality corresponding to them is in fact *within ourselves.* Accordingly, the spiritual pupil must be mature enough at this first level not to demand palpable realities but to regard these pictures as the right and necessary thing. But *within* this world of pictures we soon become acquainted with something new. Our *lower self* is only present before us as mirrored portrait; but within this portrait or reflection appears the true reality of the higher self. From the picture of our lower personality emerges the form of the spiritual I; and only from the latter are spun the threads to other, higher, spiritual realities.

And now the time arrives to use the two-petalled lotus in the regions of the eyes. If this starts to move, a person becomes able to connect their higher I with superordinate spiritual beings. The streams which issue from this lotus flower move toward higher realities in a way that is fully conscious for the person concerned. Just as light makes physical objects visible to our eyes, so these streams render the spirit beings of higher worlds visible to us spiritually.

By immersing ourselves in very specific thoughts, which the esoteric teacher imparts to the pupil in their individual tuition, the latter learns to set in motion and direct the currents of the lotus flower in the eye region.

At this stage of development, the value of sound judgement and clear, logical schooling becomes apparent. We need only consider that the higher self, which hitherto slumbered in us germinally and unconsciously, is born to conscious existence. It is not merely figurative, but literally true, to say that this is a *birth* in the world of spirit. And the being who is born, our higher self, must come into the world with all the organs and potential necessary to thrive. Just as nature has to see to it that a child is born with well-formed eyes and ears, the laws of our own self-development must ensure that our higher self comes to birth with the necessary capacities. And these laws, which themselves govern development of the spirit's higher organs, are none other than the healthy laws of reason and morality in the physical world. Just as the child develops in the womb, so the spiritual human being develops within the physical self. The health of the child depends upon the normal action of natural laws in the womb. The health of the spiritual human being is in the same way determined by the ordinary laws of reason and morality. No one can give birth to a healthy higher self if they do not first live and think in a sound, healthy way in the physical world. A life that accords with nature and reason is the foundation for all true spiritual development. Just as the child in the womb is already living in accordance with natural forces, which they perceive with their sense organs after birth, so the higher self of the human being is already living according to the laws of the world of spirit during physical existence; and as a child acquires the forces they need through an instinctive sense of life, a person does the same with the forces of the spiritual world before their higher self is born. In fact, we *must* do so if this higher self is to be born as a fully developed entity. It would be wrong for someone to say they refuse to accept the teachings of mystics and theosophists until they themselves are clairvoyant. To live by this precept would mean never developing higher perception. Such a person would be in the same condition as a child in the womb who refused the natural developmental forces coming from the mother, preferring to wait until they could procure these for themselves. Just as the foetus has an instinct of the rightness of what is nourishing it, so similarly a person not as yet clairvoyant senses the truth of the teachings of mystics and theosophists. There is a kind of insight into these teachings founded on a sense of truth and clear, sound reason, even if a person does not yet have the ability to perceive spiritually. We first have to acquaint ourselves with mystic knowledge, and prepare ourselves for seership through this learning process. Someone who became a seer before learning in this way would be like a child born with eyes and ears but without a brain, and therefore unable to make head or tail of the whole world of tones and colours.

What has therefore first been illuminating for someone through their reason and intellect later becomes a pupil's own first-hand experience at the stage of esoteric schooling described, as direct knowledge of the higher self. The pupil learns to perceive that this higher self is connected with spirit beings of a higher kind, and forms a whole unity with them. We therefore see how the lower self originates in a higher world, and we become aware that our higher nature lives on beyond our lower. Thus we can distinguish our transient nature from our eternal one. This means nothing other than learning to understand, first hand, that the higher self is embodied (incarnated) in a lower principle. We come to see that we are embedded in a higher spiritual context, and that our attributes, our destiny, are determined by this context. We learn to perceive the *law of our life*, karma. We recognize that our lower self, in its present form of existence, is only one of the forms that our higher nature can assume. And we acknowledge the possibility that our higher self can work upon us to render us ever more perfect. At the same time we can come to see why such great differences exist between people in regard to their degree of development: there are people who have advanced to a higher level than we have, who have already reached stages that we have not yet passed through; and we recognize that the teachings and actions of such people have their source in inspirations from a higher world. We owe such insights to our own first glimpse of this higher world. The 'masters of wisdom', as they are called, the 'great initiates of humanity' start to become actuality for us.

These are the gifts that the esoteric pupil owes to this stage of their development: understanding of the higher self, of the teaching of incarnation or embodiment of this higher self in a lower; of the law according to which life in the physical world is governed by spiritual realities and contexts—the law of karma; and finally also of the life of great initiates.

We can therefore say that a pupil who has reached this level no longer succumbs to any *doubt*. Previously they acquired a belief founded on reason and healthy thinking, but now this belief is replaced by full knowledge and unshakeable insight.

In their ceremonies, sacraments and rites, great religions have provided outwardly visible reflections of higher spiritual occurrences and entities, and we can only fail to perceive this if we do not yet fathom their profundities. Once we can see into spiritual reality ourselves, we can also come to understand the great significance of these outwardly accomplished rites. And then religious services become for us a reflection of our connection and dialogue with the superordinate world of spirit. . . .

Thus we see in what way the esoteric pupil has really become a new person by attaining this stage, only gradually maturing to the point of governing the *true higher life element* (the 'kundalini fire' as it is known) through the currents of their etheric body, and thus gaining a high degree of freedom from their physical body.

(Lucifer-Gnosis, April 1905)[87]

Once the esoteric pupil has succeeded in attaining this life in their higher I then—or in fact already while acquiring higher consciousness—they are shown how to awaken to existence the 'kundalini fire', as it is known, within the organ created in the heart region, and conduct it through the currents characterized in previous issues. This kundalini fire is an element of higher substance issuing from the said organ and streaming in luminous beauty through the revolving lotus flowers and the other channels of the developed etheric body. It radiates from there outward into the surrounding world of spirit and renders it spiritually visible in the same way that sunlight falling upon objects from without makes them physically visible.

How this kundalini fire is engendered in the heart organ can only be disclosed in esoteric schooling itself. This understanding is a subject of esoteric schooling itself. Nothing is communicated publicly about it.

The world of spirit only becomes clearly perceptible as objects and beings to someone who in this way can send the kundalini fire through their etheric body and into the outer world in order to illumine such objects. From this we can see that full awareness of an object of the world of spirit can only arise when a person themselves casts the light of spirit upon it. In truth, the I that engenders this kundalini light is not within the physical human body at all but, as we have shown, outside it. The heart organ is only the place where a person kindles this spiritual fire from without. If we did not do so here but elsewhere, the spiritual perceptions thus arising would have no connection with the physical world. But we do need to relate all higher spiritual elements to the physical world, and by so doing allow them to work into the latter. The heart organ is precisely what enables the higher I to make the sensory self into its instrument, and the place from where this is governed.

Now the feeling a spiritually developed person has toward the things of the world of spirit is different from that of the sensory person toward the physical world. The latter feels located in a particular place in the sense world, and the objects they perceive to be 'outside' them. The spiritually evolved person, by contrast, feels themselves to be one with the spiritual object of their perception, as if dwelling 'within' it. Indeed, they wander from place to place in the spiritual realm, and this is why such a person is called a 'wanderer' in the language of spiritual science. Really they are not at home anywhere, at first. If they remained in this wandering condition, however, they could never really determine any object apprehended in the spiritual realm. In the same way that we determine an object or location in physical space by starting from a certain point, so must we proceed also in the other world. There too we must seek some vantage point, which we first study very carefully, and take possession of spiritually. In this place we must establish a spiritual dwelling place before relating everything else to it. Likewise a person living in the physical world sees everything in terms of the thoughts they bring with them from their physical homeland. A Berliner will inevitably describe London differently from a Parisian. However, our spiritual home is different from our physical abode—we are born into the latter without our say-so, and during our youth instinctively absorb a whole range of ideas which we subsequently use involuntarily to shed light on everything. But we ourselves form and create our spiritual home in full consciousness. And for this reason also we use it in full, bright freedom as the basis of our judgement. In the language of spiritual science, this creation of our spiritual home is called 'building a lodge'.

Spiritual vision at this stage initially encompasses spiritual counterparts of the physical world, in so far as these counter-images lie in what we call the 'astral world'. In this world is to be found everything of the nature of human drives, feelings, desires and passions. You see, all the sensory things surrounding us also possess forces that have an affinity with human forces. For instance, a crystal acquires its shape through powers that, to higher vision, appear like drives or impulses active in a person. Through similar forces the sap is driven through the plant, the blossoms open, and seed capsules are brought to germination. All these forces acquire form and colour for our developed organs of spiritual perception, just as the objects of the physical world reveal form and colour to our physical sight. At this stage of development, the spiritual pupil sees not only a crystal or plant before them but also the spiritual forces I have been speaking of. And they see animal and human drives not only in the physical expressions of the latter but also directly as entities, just as we see tables and chairs in the physical world. The whole world of instinct, drive, desire and passion in an animal or human being becomes the astral cloud or aura in which the creature or person is enveloped.

At this stage of development, the clairvoyant also perceives things mostly, or entirely, unavailable to sensory apprehension: the astral difference for instance between a room that is filled largely with low-minded people and one filled with those of good intent or high ideals. In a hospital not only the physical but also the spiritual atmosphere is different from that of a dance-hall. A trading city has a different astral air from a university town. Initially the perceptions of a person who has become clairvoyant will not be greatly developed for such things, and such apprehensions will be more or less vague and dreamlike. But gradually the clairvoyant will awaken fully to such things too.

The highest achievement of the clairvoyant who has attained the degree of vision here described is to become aware of the astral counterpart to animal and human drives and passions. A loving action is accompanied by a different astral phenomenon from one fuelled by hatred. A frivolous desire is accompanied by an ugly astral counterpart, a feeling directed to higher things by a beautiful one. These counter-images can only be seen faintly during physical human life, since their strength is impaired by life in the physical world. . . .

Yet despite these counterparts or counter-images being weak while we are physically alive, they do exist, and accompany us as predisposition into kamaloka, as the tail accompanies the comet. The clairvoyant can see them by reaching the necessary stage of development.

In such experiences, and in all related ones, the esoteric pupil lives in the stage of development that has been described, and is not yet able to rise to higher experiences. From here on the pupil must rise still higher.
(Lucifer-Gnosis, May 1905)[88]

Imaginative knowledge is achieved by developing the lotus flowers out of the astral body. By means of exercises undertaken to achieve Inspiration and Intuition, particular movements, forms and currents not previously present arise in the human etheric or life body. These are in fact the organs which enable us to 'read the hidden script' and which bring within the reach of our capacities all that goes beyond this. Supersensible perception observes the following changes in the etheric body of a person who attains Inspiration and Intuition. In the region that roughly approximates to the physical heart, we become aware of a new centre in the etheric body, which configures itself into an etheric organ. Movements and streams pass from there in the most diverse ways to the various parts of the human body. The most important of these streams pass to the lotus flowers, permeate them and their separate petals and then pass on beyond the body, pouring out like rays into external space. The more highly developed a person is, the greater is the periphery around them in which these currents can be perceived. But in right schooling, the centre in the region of the heart is not developed at the very outset; it must first be prepared. There first arises an interim centre in the head which then shifts downward to the larynx, and finally is transposed to the region of the physical heart. If development were to be irregular, it would be possible for this organ in question to form immediately in the heart region, but the risk of this would be that, instead of coming to calm, sober supersensible vision, a person would become a utopian and fantasist. In the course of further development, the esoteric pupil comes to the point of rendering the configured currents and structures of their etheric body independent of the physical body, and using them autonomously. The lotus flowers here serve us as instruments by means of which we move the etheric body. Before this happens, however, particular currents and rays must have formed in the whole periphery of the etheric body, enclosing it as it were in a fine network and rendering it a self-enclosed entity. Once this has happened, the movements and currents occurring in the etheric body can touch into, and connect with, the outer soul-spiritual world, so that outer occurrences of spirit and soul and inner ones (in the human etheric body) can flow into each other. At this point a person can consciously perceive the world of Inspiration. This form of cognition arises differently from cognition of the physical sense world. In the latter we gain perceptions through the senses, and then form ideas and concepts from these perceptions. In knowledge through Inspiration it is different: what we come to know here is directly present for us in a single act. There is no reflection that *follows* perception. Whereas in physical sense perception we only form a concept after the event, in Inspiration this is one with the perception itself. If, therefore, we had not first developed the network in the etheric body as

I described, we would flow out entirely into our soul-spiritual environment and be unable to distinguish ourselves from it. *(Occult Science, an Outline, 1910)*[89]

In our physical body we have this vertical spine with the spinal cord, and in the etheric body we have a confluence, a streaming together as I just described it, in a kind of counterpart to the spine—though in relation to the physical body this latter lies frontally. Whereas nerves issue from the physical spine, as do the ribs likewise, these rays and currents in the etheric body do not emanate from, but stream together in this counter-spine with everything they contain, at the front of the human etheric body. This creates an extraordinarily beautiful and magnificent, mighty etheric organ, manifesting as a glittering, luminous, resounding entity and discharging itself in all kinds of warmth effects, but at the same time also in inward utterance. This becomes apparent especially while a person is asleep. And if we examine it more carefully, we can certainly gain a sense of how this organ infuses what I have characterized as the various lotus flowers (since such things must be described in as vivid and tangible a way as possible). And so you can see that this organ, configuring itself through what flows together from the etheric body, and then, together with the currents of the astral body, forming the lotus flowers, enables a person to further their connection with the outer, astral, cosmic world.

(Stuttgart, 2 May 1923)[90]

7. The Reversal in Thinking and Will

Activity: will

Passivity: thinking

Passive thinking is *observing*, i.e. reflecting a content separate from it.

Active will is action, i.e. realizing a content of our own.

At the moment the kundalini is awoken, passive thinking becomes active, and the active will passive.

We can describe the moment of awakening by saying that our *essential being* acquires an active, i.e. productive, thinking and a passive, i.e. receptive, will.

(Handwritten note, undated)[91]

Such meditation, practised as an essential inner, spiritual undertaking, increasingly develops our awareness of an 'inner human spirit' that can live, perceive and move spiritually with complete detachment from the physical organism. This independent human spirit arose for me through meditation, and greatly deepened my capacity for spiritual experience. That sensory perception arises through the organism is easy enough to ascertain in the kind of self-observation that encompasses such perception. But mental and ideal apprehension is also still dependent on the organism. Self-examination teaches us this: in sense observation, each act of perception is tied to the organism; in ideal, mental apprehension, each *single* act is entirely independent of the physical organism, but the fact that such apprehension can be enacted by us at all is due to the *general* fact of living within the organism. In the third type of cognition it is true to say that it can arise only through and in the human spirit, when the latter liberates itself from the physical organism to such a degree that it is as if this organism were not present at all.

Awareness of all this developed for me under the influence of the meditative life I have been describing. I was able for myself to fully refute the view that in such meditation one succumbs to a kind of auto-suggestion that gives rise to any subsequent spiritual perception. I had in fact been able to convince myself of the truth of spiritual experience with the very first ideational apprehension; truly the very first, not merely an apprehension *sustained* by meditation, but of the kind, rather, that *initiated* it. Just as, in reflective awareness, we can ascertain truth very accurately, so I had done this already in the matter under consideration here before there could have been any possibility of auto-suggestion. Thus what meditation achieved could only have been an experience of something whose reality I was already fully capable of checking and testing *before* having this experience.

All of this, connected with the inner reversal in my soul, related to a type of self-observation whose outcome, along with what I have here described, assumed great significance for me.

I felt how the intellectual, ideal nature of my life hitherto receded in a certain manner, to be replaced by the element of will. For this to happen, the faculty of will must be able to refrain from all subjective volition in the development of knowledge and perception. The will increased to the degree that ideation decreased. And the will also took over the spiritual perception that previously had been accomplished almost exclusively by ideation. I had already recognized that the division of soul life into faculties of thinking, feeling and will is only of limited application. In reality, thinking also encompasses feeling and will, though thinking predominates. In feeling, thinking and will are also at work; in will, thinking and feeling likewise. Now I began to experience how will absorbed a greater degree of thinking, and thinking of will.

On the one hand, meditation leads to apprehension of the spirit; on the other, such outcomes of self-observation lead to inner strengthening of the human spirit in its life independent of the organism, and to the consolidation of its being in the world of spirit—in the same way that our physical existence is consolidated in the physical world. The difference here, as we can become aware, is that strengthening of the human spirit in the world of spirit is immeasurably enhanced when the physical organism does not constrain it, whereas anchorage of the physical organism in the physical world gives way—at death—to decay, at which point the human spirit no longer sustains *this* kind of consolidation.
(Autobiography, 1925)[92]

8. Specific Aspects of Kundalini Schooling

At the second level [of the path], the inner light, kundalini, starts to shine forth as the spiritual sun, illumining the things of the higher world in the same way as the outer sun illumines the things and creatures of the sense world. Then comes the third level, at which the 'true I', world-encompassing self-awareness, awakens; and now it becomes possible to receive the key to true knowledge.

(Lucifer-Gnosis, May 1905)[93]

Immerse yourself entirely in the thought:

Impersonal higher self

It is not a matter here of contemplating something pre-scribed by anyone else, but of trying to form the best idea of the 'higher self' that one's degree of self-development enables one to.

We should harbour this thought as if positioning it roughly at the place in the head's interior where the P (pineal gland) is located. Shift consciousness there for a while, and fill it entirely with the above thought of 'impersonal higher self'. Thus for a while imagine that your own being has been compressed into the P, and that you yourself are this thought there. Banish everything else from your mind.

Having done this for a while, guide this same thought slowly from P down in a line to the beginning of the spinal cord, roughly where the brain passes over into the spinal cord. Then lead it on further, down to a point we call K

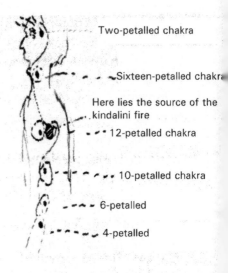

This physical body is built up through the forces of the astral body, which creates the sense organs. These—the eyes—see objects by means of outer sunlight.

In the astral body itself we must distinguish a second half [drawing] like the other pole of a magnet.

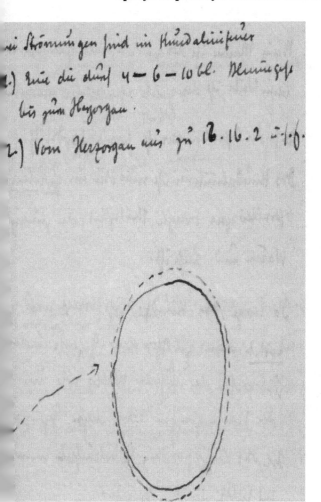

The kundalini fire has two streams:

1) One that passes through the 4—6—10-petalled lotus
   flowers to the heart organ
2) From the heart organ to the 12—16—2-petalled lotuses
   and so on.

In a man, the second astral body is feminine;
In a woman, the second astral body is masculine.
That is, the astral body is hermaphrodite.
The kundalini fire is the activity, initially warmth and light, aroused in the *second* astral body.

Until the kundalini fire is kindled, we *feel our way* through the things and beings of the higher world, as in the night between physical objects. Once the kundalini fire has been aroused, we ourselves illumine the things there.

(Notebook entry, 1905/1906)[95]

(kundalini). Having imagined that we have there imbued the thought with kundalini power (spiritual fire), we lead it slowly upward again along the spinal cord to a point in the interior of the back of the head, roughly at the place of the small brain, Point B (occiput). Now we lead the thought (imp. high. self) from this point, in two lines, to the two eyes, and then allow these to radiate out into infinite space. Then we draw them in through the two eyes again and lead them back to Point B. We do this again but now leading the thought from B to the two ears, and from there letting it stream out again into infinite space, then lead it back through the ears to B once more.

After picturing us leading the thought of imp. high. self twice through the cosmos and filling it with the latter's content, we lead the thought, thus enriched again, from B down through the spinal column to K, imbue it there in imagination with the spiritual fire, and now, *very slowly*, (so slowly that the time taken from K to the point of the larynx will be about 20 minutes) up to the throat at the level of the larynx. And there we now think this intensively:

I am not you.

I is the thought of the higher self after all the paths it has taken as described above.
You is the ordinary I, with which we do not, at this moment, identify ourselves.
(Handwritten note, August 1906)[94]

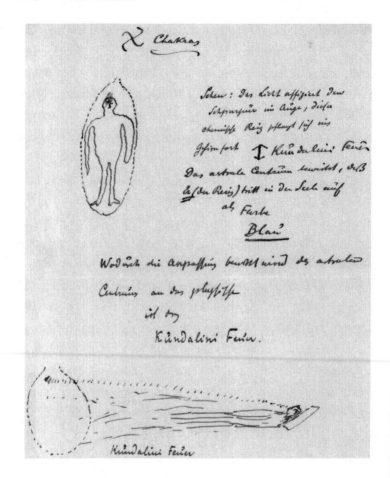

Chakras
Seeing: light invokes the rhodopsin in the eye, and this chemical
stimulus is reproduced in the brain ↑
                                    ↓ kundalini fire
The astral centre means that it (the stimulus) appears in the soul
as colour
blue
What brings about the astral centre's adaptation to the physical
is the
kundalini fire
(handwritten note, undated)[96]

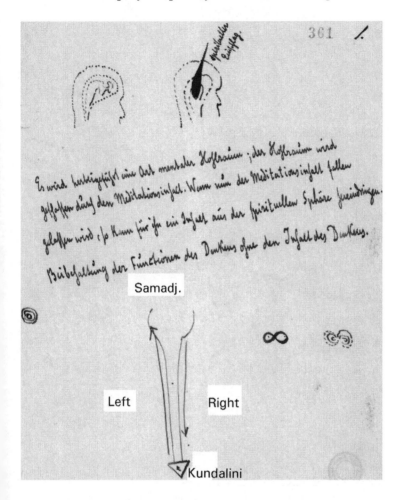

A kind of empty space in the mind is created; the empty space is /
created by the content of meditation. When we end the
meditation / a content from the spiritual sphere can enter in its
place. / Retaining the functions of thinking without the content of
thinking. /

362

Activity: will / passivity: thinking
Passive thinking is *observing*, i.e. depiction of a content outside oneself. / Active will is action, i.e. realizing a content belonging to oneself.

At the moment when kundali is awoken, / passive thinking becomes—active / and active will—passive

We can describe the moment of awakening by saying that the *being* acquires an / active, i.e. productive, thinking, and a passive, i.e. receiving, will.

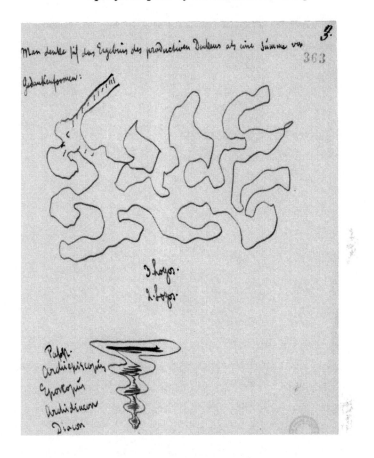

We can think of the result of productive thinking as a sum of thought forms:

3rd Logos
2nd Logos

Pope
Archbishop
Bishop
Archdeacon
Deacon
(Handwritten note, undated)[97]

Try to imagine a ray of red light that enters the brain via the left eye (at *a*):

This passes through the head to the right side of the spine (at *b*); then in spirals around the spine (*c, d, e, f, g, h*):

As it spirals, let it change into *yellow* and then *green*:

Then lead it back in spirals around the spine, letting it become *blue* and then *violet*; as a violet ray it arrives at a point *c*, which is as far left of the spine as *b* was to the right of it before; then let it pass through the head and emerge from the right eye again as a violet ray (at *d*).

This exercise should be done slowly, taking 10–12 minutes.

Before doing this exercise, meditate on this thought: the line AB, running vertically through the spine, represents the unconscious I; after the exercise, meditate on the thought that this same line now represents the I of higher consciousness.

This exercise should be done on Sunday, Monday and Tuesday, and the normal exercises on the four other days of the week: — — — — .

Commentary:
By incorporating these exercises into our meditation, we establish rhythmic contact with certain macrocosmic forces. There are always, simultaneously, old forces present in the cosmos, which were once in existence, and those that one day will be in existence, and so today are only germinally present. All forces at a certain level are ordered such that they flow into the microcosm (the human being) in spiral form.

In the red part of the ray we have the Saturn forces
In the yellow part of the ray we have the Sun forces
In the green part of the ray we have the Earth forces
In the blue part of the ray we have the Jupiter forces
In the violet part of the ray we have the Vulcan forces
(The Moon and Venus forces are not included, since they would cause a retardation of evolution.)

By incorporating these forces into us through the meditation described, we will gradually come to feel the actual motions of the two-petalled lotus flower, and will find ourselves in possession of spirit hands that can touch spiritual beings.
(Meditation given to Edouard Schuré, around 1907)[98]

1. Observe yourself from without such that you draw a line, like a colourless ray of energy, from the crown of the head descending through the spine; and along this line let the following thought run: *From here your being*

2. Observe yourself from without such that you draw a line, like a blue ray of light, between the eyebrows, winding in

imagination snakelike around the first ray of energy; and along this line let the following thought run: *Thus my seeing*

3. Observe yourself from without such that you draw a line, like a dull tone (*o* or *oo*), through the larynx, winding in imagination snakelike around the first ray of energy; and along this line let the following thought run: *Through this my strength*

(Handwritten note, around 1907)[99]

> More radiant than the sun
> Purer than the snow
> Finer than the ether
> Is the self
> The spirit in my heart
> This self am I. I am this self.

(Transcribed for Michael Bauer, end of 1904)[100]

Please do the following for the first few weeks:

1. A morning meditation, consisting of this:

Raise your feeling to the higher self. It is less a matter of instructing yourself about the higher self in some theoretical way than of having a very vivid sense and feeling of the higher nature within you. Picture the ordinary self as a vessel containing and encompassing this higher nature; in other words, imagine this latter present in the lower self as its *core*. Once you have transposed yourself into this feeling, speak a kind of prayer to the 'higher self' in the following words (not aloud but inwardly):

More radiant than the sun
Purer than the snow
Finer than the ether
Is the self
The spirit in my heart
This self am 'I'. 'I' am this self.

Do not let any other thought interfere as you picture this very precisely. You should feel only the soul's gaze directed toward the higher self. The words of the lines above should gradually give you a wonderful sense of strengthening. You will feel as if lifted out of yourself. Gradually you will feel as if the soul is growing wings. This is the beginning upon which you will then build further. This should last 2–3 minutes.

2. Then enter into deep contemplation of the first phrase in *Light on the Path*: 'Before the eyes can see, they must become incapable of tears.'

Do not allow any other thought to enter your soul. Let this thought fill you entirely. The meaning of it must strike each person suddenly, like lightning. This will happen without doubt one day, if one has the necessary patience. For several minutes, complete stillness must hold sway within you; and in this stillness you must be as if blind and deaf to all outward sense impressions, and all memory pictures. Do this, again, for 2–3 minutes.

3. Surrender in devotion to what you revere as the highest nature of the divine. The important thing here is the *mood* you invoke. Inmost reverence and yearning for union with this divine nature.

(Transcribed for Camilla Wandrey, end of 1904)[101]

9. Transforming Physical Love and the Division of the Sexes

That the soul assumes a male or female body is due to the fact that, in the evolution of outward earth nature, one or the other is urged upon it. As long as substances had not yet solidified, the soul could subject these substances to its own laws. The soul thus made the body an expression of its intrinsic nature. But once substance had grown dense, the soul had to submit to the laws that outward earth nature impressed upon it. While the soul was still able to hold sway over substance, it shaped the body neither as male nor female but endowed it with attributes that were both at once. The soul, you see, is both masculine and feminine, bearing both these natures within it. Its masculine element is related to what we call *will*, its feminine to what we call *thought*.

Outward earth development has led to a one-sided configuration of the body. The male body has assumed a form determined by the element of will, while the female body is shaped more by that of thought. And thus it has come about that the dual-gendered male-female soul inhabits a single gendered body, either male *or* female. In the course of evolution, therefore, the body acquired a form determined by outward earth forces, and henceforth the soul was no longer able to pour its whole inner strength into this corporeal vessel. It had to retain something of this strength within, only letting a part of it flow into the body.

In reading the Akashic Records we perceive the following.

In ancient times, human forms appear before us: soft, pliable, very different from later ones. As yet they still bear within them male and female nature equally. As time passes, substances grow more dense; the human body emerges in two forms, one of which resembles what will later become the man, the other, the woman. Before this distinction emerged, every person could produce a new one. Fertilization was not an outward process but something that occurred within the human body alone. But when the body became male or female, it lost this capacity of self-fertilization. It had to interact with another body to bring forth a new human being.

The division of the sexes occurs as the earth acquires a particular degree of density. The density of matter partly underpins the power of reproduction. And the part of this power that remains active needs to be complemented from without, by the opposite power from another human being. But the soul in both man and woman has to retain part of its former power within it and cannot employ it in the outer, corporeal world. And this portion of power or energy now turns inward in us. It cannot outwardly manifest, and therefore it becomes free for inner organs. And here an important moment in human evolution arises: what we call spirit, the capacity of thinking, was not previously able to find a seat in human beings, and this was because it would not have found any organ as its instrument. The soul directed all its strength outwards in order to develop the body. But now the power of the soul that finds no outer employment can connect with the power of the spirit. And through this connection organs develop in the body which will later render us thinking human beings. Thus we were able to use a portion of the power we once used to reproduce, to perfect our own being instead. The power by means of which humanity configures a thinking brain is the same as that used in primordial times in self-reproduction. The price of thinking was the division into two sexes. When people ceased fertilizing themselves, and instead fertilized each other, they were able to turn a part of their productive force inward and become thinking creatures. Thus the male and female body each outwardly represent an imperfect configuration of the soul, but because of this they acquire greater inner perfection.

This transformation happened very slowly and gradually. Alongside the old dual-gendered human forms, the later, one-gendered forms arose.

When human beings become beings of spirit, this is again a kind of fertilization. The inner organs that could be built up by the excess, unused soul power are fertilized by the spirit. The soul is intrinsically hermaphrodite, both male and female, and in ancient times it structured its body accordingly. But later it can only shape the body such that it must interact outwardly with another body, at the same time acquiring the capacity to interact with the spirit. In the external world, henceforth we are fertilized from without, while in our inner world this occurs from within, by the spirit. We have to recognize that the male body has a female soul, and the female body a male soul. Our inner one-sidedness is now balanced out by fertilization through the spirit, which revokes it. The male soul in the female body, and the female soul in the male body again become dual-gendered through this fertilization by the spirit. Thus, while man and woman are different in their outer form, within them the soul imbalance is redressed to create a harmonious whole. Within us spirit and soul merge to create unity. The spirit exerts a feminine influence on the male soul in the woman and thus renders it both masculine and feminine; and it exerts a masculine influence on the man's female soul, thus likewise making it both masculine and feminine. The hermaphrodite nature of the human being in pre-Lemurian times has thus withdrawn into our interiority.

And so we see that our higher inner nature has nothing to do with man and woman. Yet our inner equality emerges from a masculine soul in the woman, and likewise from a feminine soul in the man. Union with the spirit ultimately leads to the equality of our nature; but before this is achieved, there is difference, and it is a *secret* of human nature that this is so. Recognition of this secret is of great significance for all spiritual science, the key to important enigmas in life. *As yet it is not permitted to raise the veil behind which this secret lies concealed...*
(From the Akashic Records, 1904–1908)[102]

We have to realize that our true inner being is independent of gender, which divides people; and that we therefore pass through both genders in our different incarnations. And now you have to consider that the Freemasons have waged an outward battle, on the physical plane, to try to ensure that all individuals incarnating in female bodies are gradually led over to masculinity, so that the male will endure beyond the female. They want it to outlast the female because this was the earlier condition. That was an ideal of the masons, but it was a one-sided ideal.

What, now, is the ideal harboured by theosophy? Through the wisdom coming from higher planes, theosophy seeks to create a human race that stands above and beyond gender. This is also why theosophy is a wisdom not differentiated into religions, not based on any particular religion but reaching back to the primordial wisdom that created the world, and replacing the wisdom that has become differentiated amongst the various religions as ecclesiastical wisdom. Theosophy needed to do this because the wisdom of priests has fulfilled its mission now. Theosophy seeks to conquer the future, to cultivate what must still emerge rather than what has already been. In a sense it is a continuation of ancient priestly wisdom, of the mysteries, yet at the same time stands in a certain opposition to it.

(Berlin, 23 October 1905)[103]

In the Paris lecture cycle I presented a view that had passed through a long period of maturation within me. After explaining the interrelationship of the aspects of our human nature in general (physical body; etheric body—as mediator of life phenomena; astral body—as mediator of feeling and will phenomena; and the 'I-bearer'), I stated that the man's etheric body is female and the woman's etheric body, male. Thus anthroposophy was able to shed light on a funda-mental, existential question that was being widely discussed at the time. Here we need only recall the book by the unfortunate Weininger, *Gender and Character*, and the poetry of that time.

But the question leads us deep into human nature. Our physical body embeds us in the powers of the cosmos in a way quite different from our etheric body. With our physical body we stand within earth forces; with our etheric body we dwell in the forces of the super-terrestrial cosmos. Issues of male and female touch on great mysteries of the world.

This discovery was one of the most seismic inner experiences I ever had. I repeatedly found it necessary to approach spiritual apprehension with staying power and patience; and then, when consciousness has 'ripened' sufficiently, one must get a grip on the ideas that appear in order to transpose the view thus gained into the realm of human knowledge. *(Autobiography, 1925)*[104]

Overcoming of physical love	=	Development of astral body Transformation into manas— Ennoblement of animal kingdom	wisdom
Making breathing rhythmic	=	Development of etheric body Transformation into buddhi— Elevation of plant kingdom	beauty
Emanation of the kundalini	=	Development of the phys. body Transformation into atma— Elevation of the mineral kingdom	power

Once all this has occurred, the mineral realm will pass over into a kind of plant realm, the plant realm later into a kind of animal realm etc. etc.: the next Round.

Following on from our previous session, we need to speak a little about the significance of the breathing process. A person usually thinks they have done much if they avoid killing living creatures, if they eat a vegetarian diet and refrain from directly killing living things. But in reality we are always indirectly complicit in killing or destroying other living creatures. Nothing could live on earth if there were only human beings there who continually exhaled carbon dioxide. Human exhalations, containing carbon dioxide, poison the atmosphere and have a ruinous effect on all life. Plants on the other hand, give off oxygen and consequently make it possible for creatures to live.

When the earth was still in the condition we call Old Moon, it had as yet no mineral kingdom. In those times the entire moon was like a kind of plant, similar to a peat moor, soft and alive. Plants lived within this plant-mineral earth; as yet there were no mineral strata, although more solid parts pervaded the softer mass, somewhat like the harder accretions of tree trunks. You could not have climbed rocks or cliffs back then—they did not exist. The more solid constituents were roughly like the woody parts of plants today. In this living plant-earth lived plants of a kind that would have cried out if you had taken hold of them, for they had sentience—they were animal-plants. Mistletoe is a throw-back to such moon plants, and therefore it can only flourish on other host plants, drawing on their life. It has retained this nature from the Moon era, and this is why it is configured quite differently and has special esoteric attributes related to the evolutionary stage of Old Moon.

On Old Moon, therefore, there was:

1. A plant-mineral realm that stood higher than today's mineral kingdom;
2. An animal-plant realm, consisting of sentient plants;

3. A human-animal realm, again at a higher level than our present animal kingdom, but lower than our present human kingdom.

On Old Moon, all creatures lived to a large degree from nitrogen. The moon was enveloped in a nitrogen atmosphere. In fact, it went under as a consequence of excess nitrogen. The mushrooms and fungi that still live on a more plant-like soil today, also contain a great deal of nitrogen and are therefore not favourable for esoteric development. They remain a kind of animal-plant like those on Old Moon.

After Old Moon had succumbed to its atmosphere it passed through a period of pralaya and evolved further again into our present earth. Then everything that was not beneficial for ongoing evolution separated off in our present moon. The moon was discharged from the earth; and now, out of the [Old] Moon kingdoms, other kingdoms evolved on earth. For our present plant kingdom to emerge, a part of the plant-mineral realm had to be pushed one level lower, and this became today's mineral world. Until this point, the world was not visible to human beings. On Old Moon they could not objectively perceive their surroundings. The mineral kingdom descended one level lower, and in consequence became objectively visible. It could only become so through solidification, which meant that for the first time it was able to reflect light. Only from that time onward was there a world visible to physical sight, and this relates to the biblical narrative of the creation of light—when God says, 'Let there be light!' Planetary bodies are only visible to us if they have descended and solidified to the mineral level. All celestial bodies visible to the naked eye or through the astronomer's telescope are therefore present as mineral. What is not mineral is transparent for physical sight, which fails to discern celestial bodies that have not become mineralized. But there are far more celestial bodies in the cosmos than those which can be physically observed.

In descending one level lower, the mineral realm radiated light for the plants. Plants do not live only in the mineral world, on the mineral earth, but also from the light reflected by this realm. In the same way that plants live from this light, so animals and human animals, physical human beings, live on the earth from the oxygen which plants emit. The animal-plants also descended another level lower, while the animals rose a level, and this is why animal creatures can live from the oxygen emitted by plants. Oxygen is the physical form of what otherwise lives in the plants as prana.

The realm of human animals also divided into two kingdoms, that is, into the two sexes. This gave rise to physical love which in turn created the bond between the two sexes and, at the same time, made it possible for human beings to evolve and progress toward spiritual cognition. Because the human kingdom divided, and physical love arose, the gods were able to evolve further at the cost of human beings; and this was because human physical love was the breath of life for the gods in the same way as plant oxygen was for humans and animals, and light reflected from the mineral realm was for plant life. A Greek legend relates that the gods live on ambrosia and nectar: this is the human love of men and women. At the same time the heart, lungs and warm blood evolved in humankind—for previously they had breathed through gills, living in an atmosphere that they could not have inhaled through lungs. The respiratory organs gradually transformed in order to be able to inhale the oxygen in the atmosphere.

The ascent and evolution of humankind now consists of us overcoming physical love. The division into two sexes was necessary for the intellect to develop in us. For this purpose our nature was divided into a lower and higher one. But what now binds the two sexes together must in turn be overcome: a stage of ascent involved in us sacrificing the forces of physical love and transforming them into higher powers. By sacrificing these lower forces, the higher element can appear in us. Secondly we must then also sacrifice the forces that we withdraw from the plant world. In the breathing process we consume oxygen, the breath of life, which plants emit. By rendering the breathing process rhythmic, and through our inner spiritualization, our breath becomes purer; it then contains less carbon dioxide, and the atmosphere around is less quickly depleted. We take less oxygen, the stuff of life, from other living creatures.

Yogis living in caves tell of such things. Their capacity to do this is due to their spiritualization, which renders their breath so pure that they can live a long time without requiring a fresh supply of air. The air around them remains pure. The more spiritualized a person becomes, the longer they can live in their own air, and the less carbon dioxide they exhale. We can actually say that a materialist does much more harm with his breath than an idealist; for this reason, materialists today cannot live without continual fresh supplies of air, whereas an idealist consumes less oxygen. In fact, continual renewal of the oxygen supply has an unfavourable effect on esoteric development. Exhalation of carbon dioxide pollutes and deadens the atmosphere. What modern physicians, naturopaths and suchlike prescribe—continual fresh air and oxygen—hinders esoteric development because a person then withdraws so much life from the plant world.

The esoteric pupil learns to master their breathing process, and by this means they can bring about moments, at least, when they do not participate in the destructive process of breathing.

The third thing pupils learn is to consciously reflect light back: they develop kundalini light and radiate it out into the world. Thus they give back to the world the light of the mineral realm.

In general people are unaware of what an important instrument they possess in their own organism: they know the whole of the rest of the world better than their organism. They usually fail to see what wonderful capacities they are capable of developing.

For a person to be able to develop their organism in the right way so as to form an instrument for their higher forces, they must devote some attention to the way in which they nourish their physical body. The physical substances we ingest are not a matter of indifference.

We can distinguish within us two different natures, a lower and a higher. We must regard as our lower nature everything belonging to our warm blood, flesh, muscles etc., while everything belonging to our spiritual organs is part of our higher nature. To cultivate higher development we should choose food that does not promote the growth of our lower nature. A person who embarks on esoteric schooling should therefore avoid everything connected with the blood, flesh and muscles. Animal flesh and blood, muscles, and parts that have hardened, the bones, are all connected with Moon evolution, thus point us back to past evolutionary stages. We should instead consume things that are connected with the earth's further advance: milk, for instance, is an animal product connected with the life process, and is therefore beneficial for esoteric development.

(Berlin, 6 May 1906)[105]

10. Breathing, the Light-Soul Process, and the New Yoga Will

Pranayama means breathing, yoga breathing, and is a very central and extensive part of oriental yoga schooling. It plays scarcely no part in Christian schooling, but more so again in Rosicrucian schooling.

What does breathing signify for esoteric development? The meaning of the breath lies already in 'not killing', 'not impairing life'. The esoteric teacher states that we continually kill our surroundings when we breathe. Why is this? We draw breath in, hold it within us, supply our blood with oxygen, then exhale the air again. What happens as we do this? We inhale the oxygen-rich air, connect it within us with carbon and exhale carbon dioxide—but this cannot sustain the life of either people or animals. We breathe in oxygen, we breathe out carbon dioxide, which is a poison, and thus with every breath we kill other creatures. Slowly we kill our whole surroundings. We breathe in the breath of life and breathe out air that we ourselves can no longer use. The esoteric teacher seeks to change this state of affairs. If there were only humans and animals, all the oxygen would soon have been consumed and all life would die. That we do not destroy the earth is due to the plants, since they accomplish the very reverse of this process: they assimilate carbon dioxide, separate the carbon in it from the oxygen and build up their structures from the former, releasing the oxygen again—which animals and humans inhale in turn. Thus plants renew the atmosphere, and without them all life would long since have been destroyed. We owe plants our life. And thus plants, animals and human beings complement each other and live in mutual reciprocity.

But in future this process will change; and since those engaged in esoteric development are beginning something that others will one day also do in future, they must overcome the habit of destructive breathing. This is pranayama, the study of breathing. In our modern, materialistic era, people always want to throw the windows wide open, and they regard fresh air as a remedy of the first order. For the Indian yogi, the opposite is true: he will seclude himself in a cave and as far as possible breathe only his own exhalations. The yogi practises the art of polluting the atmosphere as little as possible by learning to fully use the air he breathes. How does he do so? This secret was once well known in the secret schools of Europe: it was called 'attaining the philosopher's stone'. To find the philosopher's stone, you must discover the secret of the breath.

At the end of the eighteenth century, something of this knowledge filtered through more generally. Much was written in public texts about the philosopher's stone, but reading these one sees that the authors themselves understood little about it, even though they were drawing on reliable sources. In 1796 an article on the philosopher's stone was published in a newspaper in Thuringia, and, among other things, stated that the philosopher's stone is something everyone has seen, that it can be found everywhere, and people pick it up for a while almost every day without knowing that this is what they have in their hands. In fact, this somewhat mysterious hint is literally true. The philosopher's stone can indeed be found everywhere.

You see, to develop its body, the plant absorbs carbon dioxide and retains the carbon from it. Humans and animals then eat the plant, assimilating the carbon again, and expelling it once more as carbon dioxide in exhaled air. This is the carbon cycle. In the future this will change: people will learn to enlarge and expand the self ever further, and accomplish for themselves what at present they leave to the plants. We have passed through the mineral and plant kingdoms, and will also return through them. We ourselves will become plant, will absorb plant existence into ourselves and accomplish the whole process inwardly. Thus we will retain carbon within us and consciously build up our body from it, as the plants do this unconsciously today. We will prepare the oxygen we need within our own organs, connect it with carbon to form carbon dioxide, and then deposit and store the carbon within ourselves. By doing so we ourselves will be able to build up our own corporeal structure, and will no longer kill off our surroundings. This is a great panoramic perspective for the future.

Now, as you know, carbon and diamond are the same substance. Diamond is crystalline, transparent carbon. Thus you need not think we will all one day be black as coal, but our body will, rather, consist of transparent carbon, carbon that is also soft and pliable. Then we will have found the philosopher's stone, for we will have transformed our own body into it.

Someone pursuing esoteric development needs to pre-figure this as far as possible; that is, we must try to relieve our breath of its destructive capacity. We must breathe in a way that makes the air we exhale useable again, so that we can breathe it in once more. How can this be done? Only by rendering the breathing rhythmic; and for this purpose the teacher gives instructions concerning breathing: we breathe in, hold the breath, then breathe out in a way that is rhythmic, albeit only for short periods. With every rhythmic exhalation, the air improves very slowly but surely. We might ask what good this is. But it is true to say that 'a stone is hollowed by a constant drip'. Every breath is a tiny drip, as it were. Chemists cannot yet demonstrate the effects of this since their methods are too coarse to measure the subtleties of substance, but the esotericist knows that this makes the breath more life-enhancing; that it contains more oxygen than under normal circumstances. Now the breath is at the same time also purified by something else, by meditation. This too contributes to the same thing, albeit only to the slightest degree: the re-assimilation of plant nature into human nature, so that we can gradually begin to refrain from killing.

(Stuttgart, 3 September 1906)[106]

You will no doubt remember my previous reference to this important fact. In my last article on the 'Social Future', in which, as it seemed, I was highlighting the importance of these things for the life of society, I also clearly pointed to the need to find something that people simultaneously grasp within them and perceive as a process of the outer world. As modern human beings we cannot achieve this by, say, reaching back to ancient yoga culture, for that belongs to the past. You see, the breathing process itself has changed. This cannot of course be proven by clinical research, and yet it is true to say that since the third post-Atlantean epoch, the nature of human breathing has altered. To put it in a rather rough-and-ready fashion, in the third post-Atlantean epoch human beings still breathed soul, whereas now they breathe air. It is not just that our thoughts have become materialistic but that reality itself has also lost its soul.

I beg you not to regard what I'm saying now as of minor importance. Please consider what it means to say that the reality in which humanity lives has itself changed—that our breath is different from what it was four millennia ago. Not just human consciousness has changed; no, indeed, soul once lived in the earth's atmosphere. The air *was* soul. It no longer is today, or rather it is so in a different way. The spiritual beings of elemental nature once more penetrate it, and we can breathe them if we practise yoga breathing. But what could be accomplished three millennia ago by normal breathing cannot be recovered now by artificial means, and this is the great illusion of those who practise oriental disciplines. What I'm describing is certainly a reality. Ensouling of the air, as this belongs to humankind, no longer exists. And this is why the beings, which I will call anti-Michaelic— of which I spoke yesterday—can penetrate the air, and through the air enter us; and in this way they enter humanity, as I described yesterday. And we can only drive them forth again if we replace yoga practice with an approach and practice that is right for us today. We must recognize how necessary it is to seek to do so. What is right and necessary can only be pursued if we become aware of our much subtler human relationship with the outer world, so that something involving our etheric body, resembling the breathing process, can occur and increasingly enter our awareness. Just as, when breathing, we inhale fresh, oxygen-rich air and exhale unusable, carbon-rich air, so a similar process is present in all our sense perceptions. Imagine you see something. Let's take a radical example: you look at a flame, you observe it. Something happens here that can be compared with breathing in, albeit in a much finer process. Then close your eyes—you can do something similar with all the senses—and you can see the after-image of the flame; and this gradually changes, and, as Goethe describes, it fades away. Besides purely physiological aspects, the human etheric body is also very much involved in the process of absorbing the light impression and in the subsequent fading of this impression. But this process contains something very, very significant. Within it is the soul element which, three millennia ago, was inhaled and exhaled with the air. And we must learn to recognize the ensouling of sensory processes in the same way that people understood the breathing process three millennia ago.

(Dornach, 30 November 1919)[107]

The reality is, rather, that a soul process occurs, passing inward from without, and is encompassed by a deeply subconscious inner soul process; and thus an interplay of the two processes arises. From without, cosmic thoughts work into us, and from within the will of humanity works its way outward. The will of humanity and the thought of the cosmos intersect at this crossing point, as the objective and subjective once intersected in the breath. We need to learn to feel how our will works through our eyes, and how, in fact, the activity of the senses gently merges with the passivity at work in the interplay of cosmic thought with the will of humanity. We must develop this new yoga will; and then something similar to what was imparted three millennia ago in the breathing process will be imparted to us. Our apprehension must become far more soulful and spiritual in nature.

(Dornach, 30 November 1919)[108]

11. The Polarity of Light and Love

But now let us address the other question: What is the intrinsic nature of soul? If, using spiritual-scientific means, we likewise enquire into the fundamental nature of soul life, then it will become apparent that—just as all matter is only compressed light—all the diverse soul phenomena on earth are in fact modifications, manifold reconfigurations, of something which, if we really comprehend its fundamental significance, we must call love. Every soul impulse, wherever it manifests, is in some way or other modified love. And if we see the human being as a being in whom, as it were, outer and inner are intertwined, interformed, then we have our outer corporeality woven of light, and our inner soul woven, in spiritualized manner, of love. Love and light are in fact interwoven in one way or another in all phenomena of earthly existence. And those who seek to understand things in terms of spiritual science will ask, first and foremost, how love and light are interwoven, and to what degree, in anything they encounter.

Love and light are the two elements, the two constituents, that pervade all earth existence: love as earthly soul existence, and light as outward, material existence.

But now we have to recognize that these two elements, love and light, which would otherwise stand side by side in the great course of cosmic existence, need to be mediated by something that weaves the one into the other. This has to be a power which, if you like, has no special interest in love, and which therefore weaves the element of light into it; which is interested only in disseminating light to the greatest possible extent, and thus allows light to shine into the element of love. Such a power cannot be a power of earth, for the earth is the very cosmos of love. The earth has the mission of interweaving love into everything. In other words, everything bound up with earth existence is inevitably in some way informed by, and interested in, love.

This is not true, however, of the luciferic beings. These remained behind at the Moon stage, in the cosmos of wisdom. It is their particular interest to weave light into love. For this reason, luciferic beings are at work wherever our interiority, which is really love-woven, comes into some kind of contact with light, wherever it is present in some form; and light is present in all material existence. Wherever we come into contact in any way with light, luciferic beings appear, and the luciferic element interweaves with love. It is by virtue of this that, through our continuing incarnations, we have entered into the luciferic element at all. Lucifer has interwoven himself with the element of love; and so into everything that is love-woven, the element of Lucifer impresses itself—and this alone can bring us something that not only makes love utter devotion but also pervades it with wisdom. And thus it is a love most inwardly pervaded by wisdom. And otherwise, without this wisdom, love would be a self-evident endowment, a power for which we could not bear responsibility.

In this way, however, love becomes the true power of the I, interwoven with the luciferic element that would otherwise only be outwardly present in matter. It is this alone that makes it possible for our inner life, which in earthly existence should come to acquire the full scope and character of love, to be pervaded by everything else that we can see as the working of Lucifer, thus leading to permeation of outward matter—so that love is not only interwoven with what light creates, but that a love arises that is imbued by Lucifer. By absorbing the luciferic element, we interweave the material existence of our own corporeality with a soul principle not only woven of love but also interwoven with the luciferic element. The love, pervaded by the luciferic element, which impregnates materiality, is a cause of illness working from within outward. And in relation to everything we previously stated as a necessary consequence of illness originating in the luciferic element, we can now say this: pain, as one such consequence—for we saw how pain follows from the luciferic element—reveals to us the workings of karmic law; and does so such that the effect of an action or a temptation originating from Lucifer comes to karmic expression in pain, and this in turn can lead to us overcoming a particular karmic effect.

(Hamburg, 27 May 1910) [109]

Undertake a meditative exercise early in the morning, soon after waking, and before any other impressions have passed through the soul. You must divert attention away from all outward impressions, remaining very tranquil and inwardly peaceful. During this time, also, let all memories of daily life fall silent; all cares and anxieties, especially, must vanish from the soul during the period of contemplation. In order to achieve this concentration more easily, you can first think of a single thought, such as *tranquillity*. And when you have succeeded in focusing your whole mind on this single thought, then let that, too, vanish from your mind, and for the next five minutes allow *only* the following five lines to live in the soul:

> In the pure rays of the light
> Gleams out the godhood of the world;
> In pure love for every being
> Shines out the godliness of my soul;
> I rest in the godhood of the world;
> I will find myself
> In the godhood of the world.

After these seven lines have lived in the soul for five minutes, focus your mind with strong resolve of will upon the point between and somewhat behind your eyebrows, as if you were living only in this point and all the rest of your body has vanished. In this act of concentration think of something that you wish to undertake. Then let this thought, too, vanish from your mind, and think only the thought, 'I *will*', retaining the focus of your concentration upon the same point.

Then do exactly the same again except that now you focus on your feet rather than the point between the eyebrows. This second part of the meditation should again last five minutes.

Then follow five minutes of reverent surrender to your divine ideal.

(Notes for Anna Haefliger, September 1906)[110]

THE PORTAL OF INITIATION

Scene 3

Benedictus (to Johannes):
The others must wait.
You have preserved your Self, my son,
As lofty forces convulsed you,
And as spiritual powers
Shrouded you in fear.
With strength your Self has battled its way through,
Even as your breast was riven by doubts
That sought to plunge you into depths of darkness.
You are my true pupil
Only from the fateful moment when
You began to doubt yourself
And thought that you were lost,
Yet found that strength upheld you nevertheless.
And I was able to give you pearls of wisdom
That brought you strength
To maintain yourself
Even when you had lost all self-belief:
The wisdom that you wrested more faithful to you
Than the faith with which you had been endowed.
Your ripeness you have proven.
You are discharged.
Your friend has passed ahead, and you
Will find her in the spirit.
I can point you on your further path:
Kindle the full might of your soul
From words my mouth now utters, that will give

The key to the heights.
These words will guide you
When nothing else that sensory eyes can glimpse
Is left to lead you.
Receive them with good will and heart's full power:
The weaving essence of light shines forth
Through breadths of space
To fill the world with being.
The blessing of love warms through
The cycles of time, invoking
The revelation of all worlds.
And messengers of the spirit conjoin
The living being of light
With soul revelation;
When human beings can wed
Their own Self with both, then will they
Live in spirit heights.
Oh spirits of which the human being has vision:
Enliven the soul of our son.
Let shine forth within him
What can illumine his soul
With spirit light.
Within him let resound
What can awaken in him
The Self to spirit's joyful evolution.

Scene Eleven

The other Maria:
I must acknowledge that a noble thing
Can only act with wholesomeness in the light,

And so my steps now turn toward the temple.
My feeling in the future must not rob
The light of love of its true consequence.

Theodosius:
Your insight gives me strength
To smooth the path for Maria's light of soul
To find its way into the world.
For souls such as your own was once,
Who did not seek to conjoin light and love,
Inevitably lost their power.

Johannes (to the other Maria):
In you I see now a soul nature which
Also holds sway within myself;
I was not able to find the path
To your higher sister
As long as warmth of love in me
Kept separate from love's light.
The offering which you bring to the temple,
Let it be recreated in my soul.
Therein let warmth of love
Offer itself up to the light of love.
(The Portal of Initiation, 1910)[111]

And we can best strengthen the warmth of soul and light of
soul that we need if we enliven it with that warmth and light
that shone forth, as the light of Christ, into the cosmic
darkness at the turning point of time. Let us vividly invoke in
our hearts, mind and will this original Christmas night that

took place two thousand years ago, so that it may help us
when we seek to bear out into the world what gleams forth to
us from the thought-light of the dodecahedral foundation
stone of love, formed in the world's image and planted within
human nature.

And so let our feeling hearts turn back toward the original
Christmas Night in Palestine.

At the crux of time
the spirit light of worlds entered
the onward earthly stream of being;
darkness of night
had held dominion;
bright light of day
streamed into human souls:
light
bringing warmth
to simple shepherd hearts;
light
that illumines
kings' wise heads.
Divine light,
Christ sun,
O warm
our hearts;
illumine
our heads;
so that good may grow
from all that we
found within our hearts,

from all that we
seek through our heads
to govern with strong purpose.
(Dornach, 25 December 1923)[112]

Spiritual powers springing from
sun-forces: shining, world-grace bestowing;
divine, creative thinking destines you
to be Michael's dress of rays.

He, the messenger of Christ, endows you with
holy world will, sustaining us;
you, the bright beings of ether worlds,
bear to human beings the Word of Christ.

So appears Michael, the Christ-proclaimer,
to patient, longing, thirsting souls:
for them your shining word streams onward
into the future age of spirit man.

You, pupils of spirit knowledge,
take up Michael's wise direction,
take up the loving Word of world will
actively into your souls' high aims.
(Last address, Dornach 28 September 1924)[113]

This too is one of the *Michael* Imaginations: he streams
through *the course of time*, bearing the light of the cosmos as
his living being, shaping the warmth of the cosmos as revelation of his own being; he surges as a *being like a world*,
affirming himself only in so far as he affirms the world, as if

guiding forces down toward the earth from all corners of the cosmos.

(Letters to members, 16 November 1924)[114]

At a time when the soul raises itself to a higher mood, on the eve of the Easter festival, this renewed experience [of the world of spirit] arises. Those who experience this feel themselves to be in the midst of a tempest, and this testifies to the fact that they are experiencing a reality not mediated by the physical body. They are raised out of the state of equilibrium in relation to cosmic forces that we normally occupy through our physical body. Their soul no longer lives this physical, bodily life, instead feeling itself only connected with the (etheric) body of formative forces that pervades the physical body. But this body of formative forces is no longer integrated into the equilibrium of cosmic forces but into the mobility of that aspect of the supersensible world that is closest to the physical world, which people only perceive when they have opened up the portals of spirit vision. Only in the physical world do forces rigidify into fixed forms that manifest in states of equilibrium. In the world of spirit, by contrast, continual mobility and flux hold sway. And the sense of being thrown off balance by such flux strikes those experiencing it as a raging tempest.

Out of the generalized sense of such a perception, *a spirit being emerges and assumes form*. It manifests in a specifically configured Imagination: the spirit being appears in a blue, star-sown mantle. In describing this being we must keep at arm's length any symbolic interpretation such as esoteric dabblers might offer as 'explanation'. The experience presenting itself here is a *non-sensory* one, which the person having it clothes for themselves and others in a picture. The blue, star-sown mantle is as little a symbol of the dark-blue night sky or similar as the rosebush would be a symbol of sunset for the ordinary mind. In supersensible perception, the soul is active in a far livelier and more conscious way than in sense perception.

In the case of the traveller to the 'Chymical Wedding', this activity is exercised by the body of formative forces in the same way that, in physical vision, this is accomplished by the sensory body by means of the eyes. This activity of the body of formative forces can be compared with the stimulus of radiating light. Such light falls upon the manifesting spirit being, and is reflected back by it. The seer thus perceives their own radiated light, and beyond its limits discerns the delimiting being. The 'blue' arises through this relationship of the spirit being to the spirit light of the body of formative forces. The stars are the parts of the spirit light that are not reflected back but absorbed by the being. The spirit being has objective reality; the image in which it manifests is a modification, which this being causes, of the radiance from the body of formative forces.

(The Chymical Wedding of Christian Rosenkreutz, 1917/18)[115]

In trying to come to a perception of the human being by means of supersensible cognition, we become increasingly aware of the antithetical nature of thinking and will activity. This contrasting quality is already apparent to the mind's ordinary, careful self-observation. But what seems to the ordinary mind to be no more than an intimation, appears brightly illumined to spiritual-scientific enquiry. The activity of thinking in ordinary life, and as employed in our customary scientific research, appears intimately bound up with processes of our bodily organization, whereas all will activity increasingly appears independent of this organization as we get further in fathoming its nature by means of supersensible cognition.

But since thinking and will activity are never distinct and separate from each other in daily soul life, the ordinary mind cannot acquaint itself with the intrinsic nature of their antithetical qualities. The ordinary mind always observes a thinking in which the will is also active, and a will pervaded by thinking, and therefore can never clearly distinguish the part played by the one or the other in our overall activity of soul. But consciousness in tune with supersensible reality is able to observe thinking and will separately from each other; and only then can we discern the intimate connection with our bodily organization of thinking active within the sense world.

(Lucifer and Ahriman and their Relationship with the Human Being, 1918)[116]

12. Transforming the Kundalini Fire into Fraternity

Now I would ask you to recognize one further thing. Once the fifth root race has come to an end, and the sixth root race is dawning, an influence will have emerged in the realm of the conscious intellect that currently, in the fifth sub-race, is still very inconspicuous, but which is nevertheless already germinal. This is something issuing from the musical principle. In the fifth sub-race, the importance of music will increasingly come to the fore. Music will no longer be merely art, but a means of expression for things quite other than purely artistic ones. And here we find something that points us toward the influence of a very particular principle on the physical plane. In the realm of music, or of what resembles music, initiates of the fifth root race will give the most significant impulses. Into the fifth root race must flow what we call the kundalini fire, and this must happen in the realm of the conscious life of the intellect, of reason. This is a power which as yet still slumbers within us but will become increasingly important. It already has a great influence today, a great importance for what we perceive through the sense of hearing. And during our further evolution in the sixth sub-race of the fifth root race, this kundalini fire will acquire great influence on what lives in the human heart. The human heart will truly have this kundalini fire within it. People will then be pervaded by a special power living in their hearts, so that, in the sixth root race, they will no longer distinguish between what serves their own good or what serves the good of all. They will be so imbued by the kundalini light that they will possess the principle of love as their most intrinsic nature.

In the seventh sub-race, while the whole of humanity will be plunged in chaos—since the root race will then be close to its demise—a small portion of people will become the true sons of the kundalini fire. They will be pervaded by all the forces of the kundalini fire; and they will provide the substance for the next root race, of those who will guide humanity's further evolution. Thus the fifth root race is heading for those heights where the divine fire, the kundalini fire, will kindle the divine principle, with sacred pathos, within human beings; and then person will no longer be divided from person but, in so far as thinking reason extends, fraternity will have been achieved. This fire will one day live in human beings. And in those who are initiated during the course of the fifth root race there lives already an intimation of this divine fire, which encompasses the power of fraternity, and which will revoke human insularity. But this is only slowly working its way through, emerging only germinally. It is still veiled and concealed by the sundering passions of human beings, the dividing powers of karma. And where it manifests here and there as precursor of a future time, it assumes a different form, a quite different character. On the plane of illusion, the divine fire is divine anger. Only when brotherliness streams through all humanity will it be divine love. But as long as it manifests, here and there, as zealous fervour, it is still divine rage, and therefore expresses itself as potent power in isolated instances, because the rest of humanity is not yet mature enough.

The poet-initiate Homer—who is said to be 'blind' because he sees inwardly—expresses this at the beginning of his epic, *The Iliad*: 'Sing, O Muse, of the rage of Achilles, son of Peleus. . .'. This is divine rage. *The Iliad* in fact portrays the manifestation of the kundalini fire on the physical plane. In the battle between Agamemnon and Achilles, anger flares up as divine rage. The legend of the Trojan war depicts how the ancient priest-king state is replaced by the worldly rule of kings, for Troy is a state in which the king is still subject to the old dominion of the priests. It is replaced by the principle of worldly cleverness. This new ascendency of worldly cleverness is very beautifully portrayed in the victory of cunning Odysseus. He is the initiate of the fifth sub-race, and his initiation is enacted through his trials and wanderings. The spirituality of the old priests is supplanted by intellectualism. This is expressed also in the image of Laocoon wound round by snakes. These snakes, a symbol of worldly cunning or cleverness, ensnare the priest Laocoon, the representative of the old spirituality.

If you follow all these threads you find that the legend of Troy in fact records a stage and context of world history. Such occurrences were portrayed in the mysteries. In the older mysteries, prior to those of Eleusis, among other things this important moment was portrayed of the dawn of the fifth root race's fourth sub-race. The Trojan war, which did actually occur, was already depicted in the mysteries before it had taken place. This sounds fantastical to anyone not conversant with theosophy. But it is a principle of the mysteries to depict not only the past, but also future occurrences. And because they prefigure the future they must be kept secret. The mysteries did not exist to satisfy human curiosity. Rather, those who were ordained to help shape the future took part in them to receive there the impulses for their mission. That is the meaning of the mysteries.

If someone were to betray a mystery therefore, it would mean that they spoke publicly of what was to happen in future. And this would inevitably cause confusion for people. Only a few advanced individuals received such an impulse, having the mission of slowly bringing humankind to the point they should eventually reach. Only the really mature individuals, who may perhaps be five hundred years ahead of their time, are capable of enduring these secrets and acting in the spirit of the mysteries. If others were to hear these things, they would immediately try to bring about conditions that humankind is not yet ripe for. Every mystery eventually enters the public domain under substantially changed conditions. Everything will at some point be revealed. The character of secrecy is due to the fact that only a few, to begin with, are ordained to prepare the future. They must lead and guide the others.

Today there are secrets that can only be revealed in the sixth root race, when quite different conditions of fraternity hold sway, which have not yet come about. Those who knew something of these facts naturally had a terrible concern that something of the mysteries might be betrayed prematurely. In the past, betrayal of the mysteries was punishable by death. The initiated priests themselves did not pass such a sentence, but those outside the mysteries who, though not initiated, knew something about them. Fear of betraying the mysteries

led to the tragic end of certain great figures. One such—
though the judgement was mistaken in his case—was
Socrates.
(Berlin, 28 October 1904)[117]

Notes

For consistency of language and style, German texts from Rudolf Steiner have been translated afresh. Thus, page references refer to the German editions, as published by Rudolf Steiner Verlag, Switzerland. However, published English translations of complete volumes, listed by the Collected Works ('GA') number are given on page 163.

1. Helena Petrovna Blavatsky. In her *The Secret Doctrine* (1888) she describes 'kundalini sakti' as follows: 'The power or Force which moves in a curved path. It is the Universal life-Principle manifesting everywhere in nature. This force includes the two great forces of attraction and repulsion. Electricity and magnetism are but manifestations of it. This is the power which brings about that "continuous adjustment of *internal relations to external relations*" which is the essence of life according to Herbert Spencer, and that "*continuous adjustment of external relations to internal relations*" which is the basis of transmigration of souls, *punar janman* (re-birth) in the doctrines of the ancient Hindu philosophers.' (Vol. I, *Cosmogenesis*).

2. Within Buddhism, knowledge and teachings about the chakras, energy systems and kundalini were preserved chiefly in the Tibetan tantra tradition. Cf. Lama Anagarika Govinda, *Foundations of Tibetan Mysticism*, 1969.

3. C.W. Leadbeater, *The Chakras*, Quest Books 2013.

4. Carl Gustav Jung, *The Psychology of Kundalini Yoga: Notes of the seminar given in 1932*, Princeton University Press 1999.

5. Lama Anagarika Govinda (1898–1985) was born in Wald-heim (Saxony, Germany) as Ernst Lothar Hoffmann, and became an interpreter of modern Buddhism and Taoism for the West. His work *The Way of the White Clouds* (1966) made him world famous, and in the 60s played a decisive part in developing public interest in Tibet and its culture. In *Foundations of Tibetan Mysticism* (1956) he deals extensively with the theme of kundalini.

6. Arthur Avalon, *The Serpent Power, the Secrets of Tantric and Shaktic Yoga*, Dover Publications 2000.

7. The theosophical periodical *Lucifer-Gnosis* was published by Rudolf Steiner in Berlin. Steiner's first spiritual-scientific journal consisted of 35 issues that appeared from June 1903 to May 1908: issues 1–7 were entitled *Luzifer* (June to December 1903); issue 8 was called *Lucifer mit der Gnosis* (January 1904); issues 9–35 were then entitled *Lucifer-Gnosis*, and appeared from February 1904 to May 1908. Between 1907 and 1909, special editions appeared with articles by Steiner alone, drawn from issues 8–35. *Knowledge of the Higher Worlds* (GA 10) was first published in book form in Berlin in 1909. Further articles by Steiner from *Lucifer-Gnosis* are contained in GA 34. On page 647 of this edition (in German), is the following editorial comment: 'Since the articles in this volume originate at a time when Rudolf Steiner was active within the Theosophical Society (1902–1912/13), we have retained the Indian and theosophical terminology that was in use in that context. At the same time, however, Rudolf Steiner coined corresponding German expressions that came into use within anthroposophy.'

8. In GA 34 (p. 68) there is an explanatory comment which states that the terms 'kundalini light', 'serpent fire', 'serpent

power' or 'inner light that illumines the world of spirit as spirit sun' were changed by Steiner in *Knowledge of the Higher Worlds* into 'spiritual power of perception' and 'an element of higher substantiality'.

9. GA 10, p. 158; original version in *Lucifer-Gnosis*, no. 23, April 1905, p. 325.

10. Ibid., p. 163–165; original version in *Lucifer-Gnosis*, no. 23, May 1905, p. 355.

11. When Steiner refers to the yoga tradition, he is chiefly citing the exercises that Patanjali calls *pranayama* in his yoga sutras.

12. GA 10, footnote on p. 94.

13. An account of the different lotus flowers and their development is beyond the scope of this book. This is described in detail in the compilation from Steiner's works, *Die Chakren. Sinnesorgane der Seele*, edited and selected with a commentary by Andreas Neider, Rudolf Steiner Verlag 2015. The account cited here is to be found in *Knowledge of the Higher Worlds*, in the chapter 'Some Effects of Initiation'. Further descriptions of the lotus flowers can be found in Florin Lowndes, *Enlivening the Chakra of the Heart. The Fundamental Spiritual Exercises of Rudolf Steiner*, Sophia Books 1998; and in Willi Seiss, *Chakra-Werk. Okkulte Unterichtsbriefe. Der Weg der höheren Erkenntnisse auf der Grundlage der Chakra-Kunde*, Achamoth 1991.

14. Undated note, Rudolf Steiner Archive NZ 362, reprinted in GA 267, p. 464.

15. GA 28, p. 326.

16. Steiner referred to the symbol of the snake on many different occasions. I cite here only his remarks in the esoteric lesson in The Hague on 25 March 1913, GA 266/3, p. 98f.

17. Lecture in Berlin, 26 September 1905, GA 93a, p. 19.

18. See Hermann Beckh, 'Der übersinnliche Organismus im indischen Yoga (Lotus-Blumen, Kundalini) im Lichte der Erkenntnis der ätherischen Bildekräfte', in *Gäa Sophia*, vol. III: *Völkerkunde*, Stuttgart, The Hague, London, Orient-Occident Verlag 1929, p. 196–212; here, p. 200.

19. GA 10, p. 140 f.

20. GA 13, p. 369f.

21. See 'Der indische Yoga im Lichte der Anthroposophie, insbesondere der Lehre von den ätherischen Bildekräften' in *Gäa Sophia*, vol. III: *Völkerkunde*, Stuttgart, The Hague, London, Orient-Occident Verlag 1929, p. 183–195; here, p. 188f.

22. Lecture in Munich on 26 August 1913, GA 147, p. 65. For more on the awakening of the lotus flowers, see ibid., p. 64–66; also Hermann Beckh op. cit, p. 196f.

23. Lecture in Berlin, 26 September 1905, GA 93a, p. 19.

24. Lecture in Berlin, 7 October 1905, GA 93a, p. 92.

25. Discussion of Annie Besant's *The Path of Discipleship*, in *Lucifer-Gnosis*, May 1905, p. 381, reprinted in GA 34, p. 528.

26. Lecture in Berlin, 26 September 1905, GA 93a, p. 19.

27. In recent times much interest has been aroused by the discovery in tombs of inscribed gold artefacts testifying to devotion to the gods. One such discovery made 25 years ago in a fourth-century woman's grave in Pelinna, Thessalia, in northern Greece, gave further clear evidence of the Dionysian mystery cult. The text, etched on gold foil in the shape of an ivy leaf laid on the woman's breast, showed her to have been an initiate of a mystery cult of Bacchus. It states that she is assured, after death, of being reborn through the 'redemptive' influence of the god Bacchus. The text of most

of the known gold foils from Pelinna can be found in Christof Riedweg, 'Initiation—Tod—Unterwelt: Beobachtungen zur Kommunikationssituation und narrative Technik der orphisch-bakchischen Goldblättchen' in Fritz Graf (ed.), *Ansichten griechischer Rituale. Geburtstagssymposium für Walter Burckert*, Stuttgart, Leipzig, 1998, p. 359–398, texts on pages 392-398. Cf. also the extensive work by Andreas Meyer, *Nietzsche und Dionysos. Eine Suche nach den Quellen des Lebens. Die Dionysos-Mysterien*, Basel, IL-Verlag 2015; and Steiner's lecture of 1 March 1906, GA 54, p. 344f.

28. Lecture in Berlin, 1 March 1906, GA 54, p. 347f.
29. Esoteric lesson in Berlin, 6 May 1906, GA 266/1, p. 152.
30. *Mein Lebensgang*, GA 28, p. 459.
31. Notebook entry in 1905/06, Rudolf Steiner Archive, NB 105, reprinted in GA 467, p. 260f.
32. Cf. Hermann Beckh, op. cit.
33. Lecture in Berlin, 29 December 1903, GA 88, p. 237f.
34. The Brihadaranyaka Upanishad, verses 3.7.1, 3.7.2, 3.7.3. Source: www.wisdomlib.org/hinduism/book/the-brihadaranyaka-upanishad/d/doc118358.html, downloaded on 5.6.2016. Sutratma is also described thus: 'The silver cord in metaphysical literature, also known as the life thread of the antahkarana, refers to a life-giving linkage from the higher Self down to the physical body; it also refers to an extended synthesis of this thread and a second (the consciousness thread, passing from the soul to the physical body) that connects the physical body to the etheric body, onwards to the astral body and finally to the mental body.' (Source: www.inner-quest.org/Glossary.htm, downloaded on 16.8.2016.)
35. Cf. entries in notebook no. 105, reprinted in GA 267, p. 460f.

Both these were probably written in 1905 in close connection with each other.

36. Lecture in Leipzig, 9 July 1906, GA 94, p. 173.

37. GA 267, p. 441.

38. In Tibetan tantra, besides the seven primary chakras, 72,000 energy channels are cited, known as *nadis*. Three of these are: *ida*, *pingala* and *sushumna*.

39. Cf. Hermann Beckh, op. cit., p. 197.

40. Arthur Avalon, *The Serpent Power*, 2nd edition, Madras 1924, p. 203.

41. Cf. Klaus Bracker, *Grals-Initiation. Anthroposophische Esoterik und die künftige Jesus-Offenbarung*, Freies Geistesleben 2009, p. 199. Hermann Beckh described this context as follows: 'Christian development, on the other hand, starts from the Tree of Knowledge, and seeks within the I, and from the zero point of consciousness, to develop the powers of the Tree of Life ('I am the bread of life'). This is also the deeper reason why the Indian yoga path can take its point of departure from the life centre whereas the western-Christian path starts from above, from thinking and the I.' (Hermann Beckh, op. cit., p. 195.)

42. Lecture in Basel, 1 October 1911, GA 130, p. 92. Cf. on this theme also Steiner's lectures in Prague on 23 March 1911, GA 128, p. 68–88 and in Munich on 25 August 1911, GA 129, p. 159–181.

43. Beckh, op. cit., p. 202.

44. Cf. Rudolf Steiner, *Die Chakren. Sinnesorgane der Seele*, op. cit., p. 20f.

45. Arthur Avalon, op. cit., p. 291.

46. *Mein Lebensgang*, GA 28, p. 327.

47. In his lecture on 20 January 1914, Steiner formulates this very

radically: 'But if we wish to enter into this point of view, a difficulty arises, a very great one. ... And this difficulty is that while we do inhabit every fibre of thought, and therefore must be most intimately acquainted with it, nevertheless most people do not have any thoughts! And usually we fail to consider this fully: that most people do not have thoughts.' (Lecture in Berlin, 20 January 1914, GA 151, p. 10).

48. GA 18, p. 134.

49. GA 10, p. 85.

50. See the chapter on insight into the nature of the self in D. T. Suzuki, *The Zen Doctrine of No-Mind*, Weiser Books 1991.

51. Cf. also Steiner's lecture in Dornach on 30 November 1919 (GA 194, p. 102–119). 'Breathing in light' via sense perception is the new way of activating the kundalini power. By 'light', Steiner here means the essential energy underlying all sense organs, not only the sense of sight. Cf. also Bracker, *Grals-Initiation*, op. cit., p. 237 ff; Baruch Luke Urieli and Hans Müller-Wiedemann, *Übungswege zur Erfahrung des Ätherischen Empathie, Nachbild und neue Sozialethik*, Dornach 1995. (*Learning to Experience the Etheric World*, Temple Lodge Publishing, 1998.)

52. For more on approaches to a spiritual psychology, see Andreas Meyer, Johannes Wagemann, Ulrich Weger (eds.): *Psychologie, Bewusstseinsforschung und Heilung im Kontext westlicher Spiritualität*, Würzburg 2016; Andreas Meyer, 'Erkenntnisgrundlagen spiritueller Psychologie', in *Die Drei. Zeitschrift für Anthroposophie in Wissenschaft, Kunst und sozialem Leben* no. 5/2015, p. 55–59; ibid., 'Anthroposophie und Psychologie. Wege zu einer spirituellen Psychologie, in *Die Drei. Zeitschrift für Anthroposophie in Wissenschaft, Kunst und sozialem Leben* 02/2016, p. 3–16.

53. Notebook entry 1905/06, Rudolf Steiner Archive NB 105, reprinted in GA 267, p. 460f. The entry dates from around 1905/06.

54. Lecture in Hamburg, 27 May 1910, GA 120, p. 193.

55. Transcribed for Anna Hefliger, end of September 1906, Rudolf Steiner Archive, NZ 7077-7079, reprinted in GA 267, p. 149ff.

56. *The Portal of Initiation*, scene 3, GA 14, p. 65–76.

57. Foundation Stone Verse for the General Anthroposophical Society, 25 December 1923, GA 260, p. 65f.

58. Lecture in Dornach, 28 September 1924, known as the 'last address', GA 238, p. 174.

59. *The Portal of Initiation*, GA 14, p. 143.

60. In a draft for the final scene of *The Portal of Initiation* in *Entwürfe, Fragmente und Paralipomena zu den vier Mysteriendramen*, GA 44, p. 162.

61. Steiner himself referred to this on many occasions. Cf. also Hella Wiesberger, 'Rudolf Steiners Lebenswerk in seiner Wirklichkeit ist sein Lebensgang', in *Beiträge zur Rudolf Steiner Gesamtausgabe* no. 51/52, 1975, p. 23; reprinted in *Archivmagazin. Beiträge aus dem Rudolf Steiner Archiv* 4, 2015, p. 241–315, here p. 292.

62. GA 22, p. 75.

63. GA 35, p. 335.

64. In the editor's commentaries in the appendix to *Seelenübungen*, vol. I, GA 267, p. 523.

65. Lecture in Berlin on 28 October 1904, GA 92, p. 102.

66. Ibid. The subsequent quotations also ibid. We can regard the path of initiation of the Templars in the twelfth–fourteenth centuries—to which Steiner often referred—as an instance of the type of initiation referred to here, and its resulting social

efficacy. Cf. for instance the lecture of 25 September 1916, GA 171, p. 116–140; lecture of 2 October 1916, GA 171, p. 195–220; lecture of 22 May 1905, GA 93, p. 143–153. Cf. also Andreas Meyer, *Die letzten Templer. Geisteswissenschaftliche Forschungen und Hintergründe zur Entstehung, Vernichtung und Fortentwicklung des Templerimpulses*, vol. II, Basel, IL-Verlag 2014.

67. GA 13, p. 344f.
68. GA 156, p. 24f.
69. GA 53, p. 255–278.
70. GA 95, p. 115–120.
71. GA 94, p. 173.
72. GA 147, p. 63–66.
73. Note from the year 1913, Rudolf Steiner Archive NZ 2466, reproduced in GA 267, p. 459.
74. Esoteric lesson in The Hague, GA 266/3, p. 98f.
75. GA 93a, p. 17–19.
76. GA 88, p. 236–239.
77. *Lucifer-Gnosis*, no. 23, April 1905, p. 325. In the book version, *Knowledge of the Higher Worlds*, the term 'kundalini fire' is replaced by 'the intrinsic higher life element' (GA 10, p. 158).
78. *Lucifer-Gnosis*, no. 24, May 1905, p. 355. In the book version, *Knowledge of the Higher Worlds*, the terms 'kundalini fire', 'power of perception' and 'spiritual power of perception' are replaced by 'the organ of perception as we have described it' (GA 10, p. 163f.).
79. Notebook entry 1905/06, Rudolf Steiner Archive NB 105, reproduced in GA 267, p. 525.
80. GA 93a, p. 91f.
81. GA 93a, p. 73.

82. *Lucifer-Gnosis*, no. 24, May 1905, p. 355. In the book version, *Knowledge of the Higher Worlds*, the term 'kundalini fire' becomes 'the organ of perception as we have described it', 'kundalini light' becomes 'organ of perception' and 'fire' becomes 'spiritual organ of light' (GA 10, p. 164f.).

83. Esoteric Lesson in Berlin, GA 266/1, p. 146.

84. GA 92, p. 102.

85. Notebook entry 1905/06, Rudolf Steiner Archive NB 105, reproduced in GA 267, p. 460.

86. *Lucifer-Gnosis*, no. 22, March 1905, p. 289–293.

87. *Lucifer-Gnosis*, no. 23, April 1905, p. 321–325.

88. *Lucifer-Gnosis*, no. 24, May 1905, p. 355–357.

89. GA 1, p. 369–371.

90. GA 224, p. 40f.

91. Rudolf Steiner Archive NZ 362, reproduced in GA 267, p. 464.

92. GA 28, p. 326–328.

93. *Lucifer-Gnosis*, May 1905, p. 381.

94. In a letter to G. Wagner, end of August 1906, Rudolf Steiner Archive NZ 6860–6862, reproduced in GA 267, p. 441–442.

95. Notebook entry 1905/06, Rudolf Steiner Archive NB 105, reproduced in GA 267, p. 460f.

96. Handwritten note, Rudolf Steiner Archive NZ 672, reproduced in GA 267, p. 462.

97. Rudolf Steiner Archive NZ 361–363, reproduced in GA 267, p. 463–465.

98. 'Meditation donné personnellement à Edouard Schuré par le Dr. Rudolf Steiner', circa 1907, Rudolf Steiner Archive NZ A 7070 (copy), GA 267, p. 444–445.

99. Handwritten note circa 1907, Rudolf Steiner Archive NZ 3219, reproduced in GA 267, p. 446.

100. Transcribed for Michael Bauer at the end of 1904, Rudolf Steiner Archive NZ 7074, reproduced in GA 267, p. 84.

101. Handwritten transcription for Camilla Wandrey, end of 1904, Rudolf Steiner Archive NZ 6912, reproduced in GA 267, p. 86.

102. GA 11, p. 74–78.

103. GA 93, p. 241.

104. GA 28, p. 458f.

105. Esoteric Lesson Berlin, 6 May 1906, GA 266/1, p. 149–154.

106. GA 95, p. 127–129.

107. GA 194, p. 108–110.

108. Ibid., p. 122.

109. GA 120, p. 192–195.

110. Rudolf Steiner Archive NZ 7077–7079, reproduced in GA 267, p. 150.

111. Excerpts from *The Portal of Initiation*, GA 14: scene 3 p. 67f; scene 11, p. 143.

112. Laying of the Foundation Stone of the Anthroposophical Society, 25 December 1923, GA 260, p. 65f.

113. GA 238, p. 174

114. GA 26, p. 116.

115. GA 35, p. 334ff.

116. GA 35, p. 409f.

117. GA 92, p. 101–105.

Sources

The following volumes are cited in this book. Where relevant, published editions of equivalent English translations are provided.

The works of Rudolf Steiner are listed with the volume numbers of the complete works in German, the *Gesamtausgabe* (GA), as published by Rudolf Steiner Verlag, Dornach, Switzerland.

GA

10   *Knowledge of the Higher Worlds / How to Know Higher Worlds*

11   *Cosmic Memory*

13   *Occult Science, An Outline / An Outline of Esoteric Science*

14   *Four Mystery Plays*

18   *Riddles of Philosophy*

26   *Anthroposophical Leading Thoughts*

28   *Autobiography*

34   *Lucifer-Gnosis; Grundlegende Aufsätze zur Anthroposophie und Berichte aus den Zeitschriften 'Luzifer' und 'Lucifer–Gnosis' 1903–1908*

35   *Philosophie und Anthroposophie, Gesammelte Aufsätze 1904– 1923*

44   *Entwürfe, Fragmente und Paralipomena zu den vier Mysteriendramen*

54   *Die Welträtsel und die Anthroposophie*

88   *Concerning the Astral World and Devachan*

92   *Die okkulten Wahrheiten alter Mythen und Sagen*

93   *The Temple Legend*

93a   *Foundations of Esotericism*

A NOTE FROM RUDOLF STEINER PRESS

We are an independent publisher and registered charity (non-profit organisation) dedicated to making available the work of Rudolf Steiner in English translation. We care a great deal about the content of our books and have hundreds of titles available – as printed books, ebooks and in audio formats.

As a publisher devoted to anthroposophy…

- We continually commission translations of previously unpublished works by Rudolf Steiner and invest in re-translating, editing and improving our editions.

- We are committed to making anthroposophy available to all by publishing introductory books as well as contemporary research.

- Our new print editions and ebooks are carefully checked and proofread for accuracy, and converted into all formats for all platforms.

- Our translations are officially authorised by Rudolf Steiner's estate in Dornach, Switzerland, to whom we pay royalties on sales, thus assisting their critical work.

, look out for Rudolf Steiner Press as a mark of quality
d support us today by buying our books, or contact us should
u wish to sponsor specific titles or to support the charity
with a gift or legacy.

office@rudolfsteinerpress.com
Join our e-mailing list at www.rudolfsteinerpress.com

RUDOLF STEINER PRESS